# READ LEARN INSPIRE

This book has been self published by the author via Kindle Direct
Publishing. Both the 50 limited editions of this book and the
standard issue will be distributed via Amazon. When purchased
through Amazon this book will be printed on demand locally to
help reduce financial and environmental costs.

First Printing, 2020

ISBN 9798688991499

Sussex Cottage, Norton Green ,Isle Of Wight  PO40 9RY

www.ReadLearnInspire.com
@ReadLearnInspire

# READ LEARN INSPIRE

A GUIDE TO THE TOP 100 SELF HELP,
DEVELOPMENT & PERSONAL GROWTH BOOKS

ALEX STEWART

# CONTENTS.

INTRODUCTION.                                    6

HOW TO USE THIS BOOK.                           10

STRATEGIC OVERVIEW.                             14

TOP 10 & RAPID REFERENCE.                       22

1. HABITS.                                      24

2. HEALTHY LIVING.                              38

3. TIME MANAGEMENT.                             58

4. MINDFULNESS & MENTAL HEALTH.                 68

5. FINANCE & BUDGETING.                         84

6. COMMUNICATION & RELATIONSHIPS.              104

7. INSPIRATION.                                122

8. MOTIVATION.                                 142

9. PURPOSE.                                    162

10. PERSPECTIVE.                               176

11. GOALS.                                     196

12. SUCCESS MINDSET.                           206

13. PRODUCTIVITY.                              230

14. ENTREPRENEURIALISM & BUSINESS.             248

15. CONFIDENCE.                                264

16. BONUS CHAPTER: INSIGHT.                    284

FINAL THOUGHTS.                                310

THANK YOU.                                     312

# INTRODUCTION.

*"The man who does not read good books has no advantage over the man who can't read them"*
*— Mark Twain*

Strong words I know, but very true. Listen, when I was 32 I could recall every book I had ever read and that wasn't for a good reason. There were only four. Two were mandatory books for my English GCSE and the other two were mandatory before enrolling into the Royal Airforce. I'm now approaching 40 years old and I've read hundreds. This is not a brag in anyway, I am not a life coach and I am not an author. I simply want to impress on you the importance of personal development and how reading some self help books can be absolutely life changing.

When I started to read books, voluntarily, I very quickly became hooked on the new knowledge and insights that I was picking up. I wanted to read as much as I could as quickly as I could. To do this I used, and still use, audio books. This works great for me as I read VERY slowly and the thought of picking up a hard copy of a book and reading it in the traditional manner practically sends me to sleep. So audio books, sometimes sped up to two or even three times the speed, have been an absolute revelation to me. After reading the books I would end up talking to anyone who would listen to me about what was in the book. Soon people started to ask what books they think they should read out of the ones I had been discussing. So I started to recommend to people the most relevant book that I knew about that I thought would benefit their situation.

After reading an increasing number of books I soon found that I started to forget which book had the information in that I was suggesting for people and so I started to write down a mini review every time I finished a book. This went on for several years and I soon found that I had several hundred of reviews. I also got a little overwhelmed with the requests for recommendations so I started a small blog site www.ReadLearnInspire.com

Then someone came up with the wise idea that I should write a book and, well as you can see, that's what I did.

So I have written this book for myself. But it's not what you think. When I say I have written for myself I mean for my younger self. You see when I started reading I thought what an incredible waste it was to have not already consumed all this knowledge at a younger age. If I had read all these books when I was 18 I can't imagine how much of a positive change it would have made. When I chatted to other people about some of the titles I had devoured they would exclaim that "surely everyone has read that book, haven't they?". Well the answer to that is NO! Because I still speak to people with varying ages and backgrounds that have never heard of some of the titles in this book. And it's no exaggeration when I say some of them will alter your life.

So to my younger self I would say reading is something you currently associate with school. School will educate you in academic subjects and provide you with a bench mark of how you are doing compared to your peers and eventually an employer will probably be curious about your academics. However , life rarely gives two shits about your grades. Once you finish your academic education, at whatever level you decide to stop, you will be responsible for educating and developing yourself. No one is going to tell you this and it will be years and years until you realise that some people have been developing their own knowledge whilst you have not. School is going to teach you academics. It's not going to teach you about life. After school, life is what matters and you will have a lot of it ahead of you.

A book containing the guide to life would be far too big and you'd need to be a lot older than me to write it. But life, and some of its challenges, can be broken down into sections or topics. Books covering these different topics can be found in the personal development and self help genre. The world of self help books can be overwhelming. There are hundreds on each topic and trying to judge the book by the cover can be very tricky. There are some that are an utter waste of time and some that you'll want to start reading again as soon as you've finished them.

So in this guide I have provided a concise summary of the best books I have personally read within the different areas of self help. I have broken the huge topic down into manageable sections and my hope is that if you, or someone you know, is struggling with an area of their life, or just wants to do even better in a given discipline, then this book will be the perfect starting point. So you can get yourself on track to where you want to go and be the person you want to be.

Each book review should help you decide if you want to read the whole book. As you now know I am an avid audiobook consumer and so everything in here is available on audible and in hard copy from major book sellers.

Everything in this book is my opinion alone, there are no paid placements or promotions so you can be assured there is no bullshit or fluff present.

If you think this guide is helpful then please pass it on to someone else. Actually buy them as copy as a gift, its available on Amazon, it will make their day and mine! If you do like the book and you put a review on Amazon then you'd would be helping other people make a better decision if this book is right for them. I genuinely mean it when I say: It's not about the money it's about the message. If reading this inspires some one else to take on reading and have a positive impact on their life then the book will have served its purpose. If you don't like the book you could burn it or you could use it to prop up the leg of a wonky table.

# HOW TO USE THIS BOOK.

The idea behind this book is to use is at a simple guide. Almost like a manual that contains information on how you can help yourself or indeed try and help someone else. So if I met my younger self I might say "Alex, I know at the moment you probably feel the last priority you have is reading but I've come across this awesome guide that has reviews of books that you might find really interesting. It is divided into handy subsections, each relating to a different subject area, and if you take a moment to look through it I think it will point you in the direction of some wisdom that would really benefit you. All the book suggestions are available in audio format and you can use the guide as a reference to suit you so you don't need to read it all the way through from start to finish".

So there is a strategic overview where all of the chapters are listed as well as a list of all the books and authors. Pick the chapter that you find most pertinent to your current situation. Then head to that chapter. What you'll find in every chapter is an introduction to the topic and how some of the concepts can really make a difference in your life. Then every book has been reviewed and after reading those reviews you can decide which book, or books, are the ones that you'd like to read fully. Feel free to make notes in this book about the other books you have read and what you'll find is that you build your own personalised guide that contains the information in it that you wanted to remember and that you thought was pertinent .

I've designed the book to be utilitarian as well. If you find you want to make notes then there is space, next to every review for this exact purpose. Making notes is scientifically proven to reinforce what it is you have leant and in this book it will help you keep track of your progress.

All of the books have a score next to them as well. In an effort to be accurate and offer a higher fidelity on my rating of the book I have given the score as a percentage, a mark out of 100. To save you time I haven't added any titles into this book that I rated at less than 70%.

The idea is to highlight, underline, note and scribble throughout this book and use it like a working manual as you progress through some of the books it recommends. With folded down corners and a well worn cover it will eventually become a guide book that you can keep coming back to again and again. You might decide to keep it private, almost like a personal journal or you may want to show it to everyone in order to pass on all the knowledge you have gained.

I have listened to every book in hear (see what I did there?) at least once and I'd listen to them all again! So every title that I recommend, via the reviews, is a title where I really feel you wouldn't be wasting your time. The self help genre is massive. It's utterly saturated with books and whilst some of them are worth their weight in gold some of them are absolutely shit. This guide will save you from wasting your time and provide you with an ever more valuable resource that you can continually go back to and build upon.

If you don't agree then by all means let me know and if there is a revision of this book I'll alter it accordingly, and even reference you in the subsequent edition!

If you make your way through the whole book and find that you run out of inspiration for new books to read then head over to www.ReadLearnInspire.com . I continue to review new books and they will be on this site weekly as well as recommendations for related podcasts and other further reading. So far the reviews are up to 380 and growing all the time.

Each book has key lessons to take away from them, but one thing that applies to all of them is taking some form of action. So I implore you to look through this guide, choose your biggest priority, read the reviews, go off and get the book, read it and then ACT upon the advice! TAKE ACTION, nothing will ever change or improve if you just sit on your fat arse and nod in agreement.

Don't be the lazy fuck that gets left behind. Should have, would have, could have means you're out of time! We all have the same 24 hours in a day and there's no reason you can't make the most of yours. I'd recommend reading all the books I have reviewed but I appreciate it takes time. We are all busy but with this handy guide at least you won't be wasting your time on woo woo books that just tell you to 'imagine money and you'll be rich'.

# STRATEGIC OVERVIEW.

## 1. HABITS

*Help with breaking the bad and starting good.*

| | |
|---|---|
| The Power Of Habit | Charles Duhigg |
| Atomic Habits | James Clear |
| Nudge | Thaler & Sunstein |
| Tools Of Titans | Timothy Ferris |
| Habits of the Super Rich | Bruce Walker |

## 2. HEALTHY LIVING

*Live well, eat well, sleep well.*

| | |
|---|---|
| The Four Pillar Plan | Rangan Chatergee |
| A Year of Living Danishly | Helen Russell |
| Get Your S**t Together | Sarah Knight |
| Ikegai | Hector Garcia |
| The Stress Solution | Rangan Chatergee |
| Minimalism | Ingrid Bjork |
| Sleep | Nick Littlehales |
| Rest | Alex Soojung |

## 3. TIME MANAGEMENT
*How to make the most of a limited resource.*

| | |
|---|---|
| Time Management | Brian Tracey |
| The One Thing | Gary Keller |
| Eat That Frog | Brian Tracey |

## 4.MINDFULNESS AND MENTAL HEALTH
*Awareness of the mind and maintaining its health.*

| | |
|---|---|
| Positive Thinking | Napoleon Hill |
| The Practicing Mind | Thomas M Sterner |
| 13 Things Mentally Strong People Don't do | Amy Morin |
| Reasons to Stay Alive | Matt Haig |
| The Search For a Balanced Life | Sanjay Burman |
| TheBullet Journal Method | Ryder Carrol |

## 5. FINANCE AND BUDGETING
*Personal finance, budgeting and learning about money.*

| | |
|---|---|
| Rich Dad Poor Dad | Robert Kiyosaki |
| How to be Smart with Money | Duncan Banytyne |
| I Will Teach You To Be Rich | Ramit Sethi |
| The Compound Effect | Darren Hardy |
| Wealth Secrets of the 1% | Sam Wilkin |
| The Automatic Millionaire | David Bach |
| Money | Rob Moore |
| The Ascent of Money | Niall Ferguson |

## 6. COMMUNICATION AND RELATIONSHIPS
*Build, maintain & get more from our human interactions.*

| | |
|---|---|
| The Five Love Languages | Gary Chapman |
| The School of Life | Alain De Botton |
| Talking to Strangers | Malcom Gladwell |
| The Chimp Paradox | Steve Peters |
| The book you wish your parents.. | Philippa Perry |
| How To Win Friends and Influence People | Dale Carnige |
| Surrounded by Idiots | Thomas Erikson |

# 7. INSPIRATION
*Some of the worlds greatest people illustrated.*

| | |
|---|---|
| Can't Hurt Me | David Goggings |
| The Greatest | Matthew Syed |
| Steve Jobs | Walter Isacson |
| Becoming | Michelle Obama |
| Total Recall | A. Schwarzenegger |
| Empire | Howard Hughes |
| The Audacity of Hope | Barack Obama |
| Winning | Alistair Campbell |

# 8. MOTIVATION
*The fire to start, keep going and NEVER quit!*

| | |
|---|---|
| Drive | Daniel Pink |
| 10X Rule | Grant Cardone |
| Tipping Point | Malcom Gladwell |
| The Dip | Seth Godin |
| How To Stay Motivated | Zig Ziglar |
| How to be Fucking Awesome | Dave Meredith |
| Be Obsessed or Be Average | Grant Cardone |
| The Alchemist | Paulo Coelho |

## 9. PURPOSE

*Helping you figure out yours if you don't already know.*

| | |
|---|---|
| Start With Why | Simon Sinek |
| The Values Factor | John DeMartini |
| Tribes | Seth Godin |
| Mans Search For Meaning | Victor Frankl |
| The Gratitude Effect | John DeMartini |

## 10. PERSPECTIVE

*Get some! No one has too much of it.*

| | |
|---|---|
| Outliers | Malcom Gladwell |
| The Monk Who Sold His Ferrari | Robin Storme |
| What Doesn't Kill Us | Scott Carney |
| Homo Deus | Yuval Noah Horari |
| David and Goliath | Malcom Gladwell |
| The Inevitable | Kevin Kelly |
| The Theory Of Everything | Stephen Hawkins |
| God is Not Great | C. Hitchens |

# 11. GOALS
*Set, track, attain.*

| | |
|---|---|
| Focal Point | Brian Tracey |
| Unstoppable | Pete Wilkinson |
| Habit Stacking | The Blokehead |

# 12. SUCCESS MINDSET
*The clues that successful people have left for you.*

| | |
|---|---|
| The Success Principles | Jack Cranfield |
| Grit | Angela Duckworth |
| The Law of Success | Napoleon Hill |
| 21 Secrets of Self Made Millionaires | Brian Tracey |
| Endure | Alex Hutchinson |
| The Obstacle is The Way | Ryan Holiday |
| Millionaire Success Habits | Dean Grizosi |
| Ego is The Enemy | Ryan Holiday |
| The Impulse Society | Paul Roberts |
| The Magic of Thinking Big | David Schwartz |

## 13. PRODUCTIVITY
*Getting more done with the most precious commodity, time.*

| | |
|---|---|
| The 80/20 Principle | Richard Koch |
| The slight Edge | Jeff Olson |
| Life Leverage | Rob Moore |
| 7 Habits of Highly Effective People | Stephen Covey |
| The Miracle Morning | Hal Elrod |
| The Four Hour Work Week | Timothy Ferris |
| Deep Work | Cal Newport |

## 14. ENTREPRENEURIALISM AND BUSINESS
*Creative and pragmatic inspirations and solutions.*

| | |
|---|---|
| Zero to One | Peter Thiel |
| If You're Not First You're Last | Grant Cardone |
| Loosing My Virginity | Richard Branson |
| Scrum | Jeff Sutherland |
| The Infinite Game | Simon Sinek |
| The Thank You Economy | Gary Veynerchuck |

## 15. CONFIDENCE
*You're probably already ready, here's your reassurance.*

| | |
|---|---|
| Failing Forward | John Maxwell |
| Start Now Get Perfect Later | Rob Moore |
| The Subtle Art of Not Giving A F**k | Mark Manson |
| You Do You | Sarah Knight |
| Anyone Can Do It | Duncan Banytyne |
| You Are a Badass | Jen Sincero |
| Trusting Yourself | MJ Ryan |
| The Imposter Cure | Jessamy Hibberd |

## 16. **BONUS CHAPTER**: INSIGHT
*Mind opening information across incredible subjects.*

| | |
|---|---|
| Black Box Thinking | Matthew Syed |
| Humans | Tom Philips |
| This is Going to Hurt | Adam Kay |
| Prisoners of Geography | Tim Marshall |
| War Doctor | David Knott |
| Checklist Manifesto | Atol Gwande |
| Countdown to Zero Hour Day | Kim Zotter |
| You Are Not So Smart | David McRaney |
| Catching Stardust | Natalie Starsky |
| 81 Days Below Zero | Brian Murphy |

# TOP 10 & RAPID REFERENCE.

Ok so if you don't have time to go through the book or don't want to dive that deeply into a specific topic then hopefully these few pages will give you the fast fix you need. Included here are my Top 10 books of all time and a Rapid Reference, my top rated book within each chapter in this book.

## TOP 10

| 1. | Rich Dad Poor Dad. | Robert Kiyosaki | P 90 |
|----|--------------------|-----------------|------|
| 2. | Atomic Habits. | James Clear | P 32 |
| 3. | Can't Hurt Me. | David Goggings | P 128 |
| 4. | Outliers. | Malcom Gladwell | P 182 |
| 5. | The Success Principles. | Jack Cranfield | P 212 |
| 6. | A Year of Living Danishly. | Helen Russell | P 46 |
| 7. | The Values Factor. | John DeMartini | P 170 |
| 8. | The Five Love Languages. | Gary Chapman | P 110 |
| 9. | The Infinite Game. | Simon Sinek | P 262 |
| 10. | Grit . | Angela Duckworth | P 214 |

# RAPID REFERENCE

| | | |
|---|---|---|
| 1. Habits. | Atomic Habits | P 32 |
| | **James Clear** | |
| 2. Heathy Living | A Year of Living Danishly | P 46 |
| | **Helen Russell** | |
| 3. Time Management | The One Thing | P 66 |
| | **Gary Keller** | |
| 4. Mindfulness & Mental Health | 13 Things Mentally Strong People Don't Do | P 78 |
| | **Amy Morin** | |
| 5. Finance & Budgeting | Rich Dad Poor Dad | P 90 |
| | **Robert Kiyosaki** | |
| 6. Communication & Relationships | The Five Love Languages | P 110 |
| | **Gary Chapman** | |
| 7. Inspiration | Can't Hurt Me | P 128 |
| | **David Goggings** | |
| 8. Motivation | Tipping Point | P 152 |
| | **Malcom Gladwell** | |
| 9. Purpose | The Values Factor | P 170 |
| | **John DeMartini** | |
| 10. Perspective | Outliers | P 182 |
| | **Malcom Gladwell** | |
| 11. Goals | Focal Point | P 202 |
| | **Brian Tracey** | |
| 12. Success Mindset | The Success Principles | P 212 |
| | **Jack Cranfield** | |
| 13. Productivity | Life Leverage | P 240 |
| | **Rob Moore** | |
| 14. Entrepreneurialism & Business | The Infinite Game | P 262 |
| | **Simon Sinek** | |
| 15. Confidence | You Do You | P 276 |
| | **Sarah Knight** | |
| 16. Bonus Chapter: Insight | Black Box Thinking | P 290 |
| | **Matthew Syed** | |

# 1. HABITS.

*Help with breaking the bad and starting good.*

You will hear mentioned, time and again, that the key to implementing any change is action. In order to implement that action it is imperative to learn the science and art of changing habits. There are countless studies that have gone into changing habits, the best way to set and adopt new habits, how to eliminate bad ones and how to ensure that the ones you want to keep can be permanently implemented. The books I have reviewed will go into some levels of depth to prove this science to you but the three key elements repeated time and again are REPETITION, ROUTINE and REALISM.

Repetition of a task, time and time again, serves several purposes. It ingrains the habit into our behaviour making it an innate like practice that requires very little thought. This removes some of the challenges of forming a positive habit like resistance to the task and difficulty. This links to routine. If you can make a habit part of a routine, that is regularly in your schedule then again it's easy to implement and persist with it. Finally realism. If a habit is very hard then it will be difficult to implement it and maintain it consistently so an easy habit will, by its very nature, be easy to adopt. Brushing your teeth is a classic positive habit that encompasses repetition, routine and realism. Smoking is a negative habit that does the same.

Once you realise that you want to make a change in your life, in any area, you will quickly fall back upon the reliance of habit forming to achieve it. So let's look at this area first and give ourselves a couple of wins up front to keep us motivated.

You may have some bad habits that you want to eliminate or you may have some good habits that you want to adopt. A good thing to consider is making small and achievable steps at first. This will avoid overwhelm and a fear of failure and at the same time a small change, being easier to adopt, will give a positive sense of feedback and reward and in doing so will encourage you to make small incremental changes to your life, a concept referred to as 'Marginal Gains or Kaizen'.

It's important to stress as well the sage advice that habits can be easy to do and equally can be easy not to do. Small, incremental, improvements repeated over a lifetime can have a phenomenal effect later on. This is an effect known as compounding that Albert Einstein once described as the 'eighth wonder of the world'. In The book 'The Compound Effect' by Darren Hardy, which I review in Chapter 5, you'll see this illustrated very well. For now though trust me that a positive habit, easy to achieve and set, will have a huge effect later on and a negative habit, even if seemingly small, will compound into an undesirable outcome that could even be catastrophic.

'The Power of Habit' and 'Atomic Habits' are going to be the best place to get started. These books will help to illustrate some of the fundamental techniques to adopt if you are hoping to engage in a new habit or eliminate or replace an old one. 'Tools of Titans' and 'Habits of the Super Rich' would be best read next to develop on top of the previous principles you will have read about. These two books are going to deal more with inspiration for new habits and will offer insight on the practices and habits that incredibly successful people have adopted. Essentially after learning exactly how to set or replace habits it is important to discover and decide which new habits you think will best suit you and your life and that's why I recommend that order. You can read them in any order, it's entirely up to you, these are merely a few suggestions to help you achieve what it is your looking for.

Another really interesting concept surrounding behavioural patterns and habits is that of 'triggers'. A trigger can be an event, an emotion, a smell or another stimulus that 'triggers' a reaction from you. Now either you recognise, utilise and control these triggers or you'll find that other people will recognise them and utilise them to control you. For instance, you walk past a bakery, you don't even see it, you just smell the air and the fresh smell of bread and pastry and suddenly you're hungry and you're in there getting your donut fix! Well if you recognise this is happening you can acknowledge that the smell has merely triggered an endorphin related memory and that you're not even hungry! Big businesses utilise this against you and manipulate your behaviour. It's no coincidence that you can smell a McDonalds often before you can see it. They are using your triggers. So in learning about habits you can identify your own triggers and you can use them for your benefit and your wellbeing.

A final word on the importance on this chapter. Almost ALL of the other books I have read and reviewed stress that developing positive habits and habit forming are one of the fundamental elements of success. This is one of the foundations of personal development and without it you will find it much harder to implement positive change. If you don't have the ability to make change consistent what you will find is the effort you put in to starting a new habit could be wasted much like the implementation of a fad diet! There are great tips in these books to make changes easier and fantastic hacks on increasing the reliability of your habits with the aide of technology. In particular look out for 'habit stacking' as great technique to adopt and enjoy discovering some of the human behavioural psychology concepts that you will be able to control.

| | |
|---|---|
| The Power Of Habit | Charles Duhigg |
| Atomic Habits | James Clear |
| Nudge | Thaler & Sunstein |
| Tools Of Titans | Timothy Ferris |
| Habits of the Super Rich | Bruce Walker |

# The Power Of Habit - Charles Duhigg

SCORE: 88%

OUTLINE: How to set, change and eliminate habits.

REVIEW: Habits have 3 stages. A trigger, a routine and a result. Keep the trigger and result but change out the routine for something else, something better, healthier, more fulfilling, more productive. In all instances the trigger is a powerful thing to identify and set into a routine pattern if you want to enforce it. A lot of links to aviation safety and the potential to transfer them into other sectors - Medical, petrochemical, construction, service - the list is endless really. This book will be a great start for someone looking to make changes in their life with a meaningful and practical way of making that change permanent.

THE INTERNATIONAL BESTSELLER

## Tiny Changes,
## Remarkable Results

# Atomic
# Habits

An Easy & Proven Way
to Build Good Habits
& Break Bad Ones

# James Clear

# Atomic Habits - James Clear

SCORE: 90%

OUTLINE: Excellent guide to positive habit change.

REVIEW: In this book the author reviews some great tips and hacks on developing positive habits. How to change out old bad habits, where and when to instigate new ones and how to identify what habits might actually work for your personality type. Learn how to build a system for getting 1% better every day, break your bad habits and stick to good ones. He discusses avoiding the mistakes people make when changing habits, how to overcome a lack of motivation and willpower and how to develop a stronger identity and believe in yourself.

There is so much valuable content in this book and most importantly, how to action these ideas. There are some topics in this book that perhaps deserve more focus, and you'll see this where a related book dedicates the whole title to said topic. However, what James does achieve is more coverage and a great content balance. I always find repetition, something the book offers, really helps to ingrain methods of habit forming so that they eventually become second nature.

MORE THAN 1.5 MILLION COPIES SOLD

# RICHARD H. THALER
WINNER OF THE NOBEL PRIZE IN ECONOMICS

and CASS R. SUNSTEIN
WINNER OF THE HOLBERG PRIZE

## *Nudge*

NEW YORK TIMES Bestseller

Improving Decisions About

Health, Wealth, and Happiness

"One of the few books . . . that fundamentally changes the way I think
about the world." —Steven D. Levitt, coauthor of FREAKONOMICS

# Nudge - Thaler and Sunstein

SCORE: 78%

OUTLINE: Improve your decisions on health, wealth and Happiness.

REVIEW: The authors look at the way humans make decisions everyday and how if more of the analytical brain was involved those decisions would be less emotional, more objective, and actually for the better. They discuss libertarian parenting and how it offers choice to children and nudges them in the right direction without forcing them to think or behave in a certain way or removing other choices. It looks at how this concept works in businesses, health care and marriage. It considers how 'choice architects', professionals who manipulate things like store layouts to influence our purchasing behaviour, can change the decisions we make and the subsequent course our lives will follow. This is an incredibly interesting book

.

# Tools Of Titans - Timothy Ferris

SCORE:90%

OUTLINE: A text book of life improving tools.

REVIEW: This book is a WEAPON! This book is not a cover to cover read and that is one of things I love about it! It's more like a life manual from a very successful podcast host that is designed to be picked up and used on an 'as and when needed basis'. It's one of the very few hard copy books I own and it sits on my night stand always within arms reach. Use the books index and the categories listed that are relevant to the change you're trying to implement. It then directs you to a page where Tim has interviewed a notable person on that topic and that experts recommendation in how to best change or improve that topic. This book is a must own! It's huge and yet slammed full of great content and something to keep forever. If you don't have this book you ARE at a disadvantage!

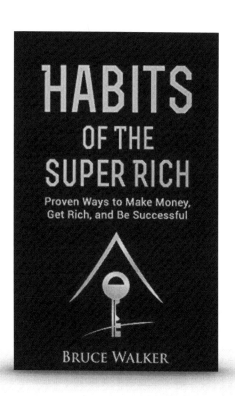

# HABITS
## OF THE
## SUPER RICH
### Proven Ways to Make Money, Get Rich, and Be Successful

BRUCE WALKER

# Habits Of The Super Rich - Bruce Walker

SCORE: 70%

OUTLINE: Habits and strategies that can have a compounding effect on your life if actioned.

REVIEW: The author essentially offers a two hour précis of several other self help books that help you to manage your time, finances, lifestyle, aspirations and relationships. The author covers chapters on habits of the rich and poor, turning thoughts into reality, developing a successful persons mindset and universal laws of success. He also looks at the power of a mastermind, which is something I can wholeheartedly endorse from personal experience, and speaks about effective ways to build a habit.

Each chapter in the book is an entire concept in other peoples writings so this will give you a good, broad insight. Other titles, that I have reviewed previously, will offer you a more in depth and richer coverage of a specific topic if that is what you prefer. Never-the- less a great refresher!

# 2. HEALTHY LIVING.

*Live well, eat well, sleep well.*

In the healthy living chapter we look at all of the things we should be doing on a daily basis but perhaps don't. This might be for a number of reasons. Some people will say, 'This is all common sense', but that is only the case if you have been educated and surrounded by healthy people that have passed on this knowledge to you. If you are not aware, for instance, that staring at a mobile device such as iPhone or an iPad last thing at night, will cause the blue element of light in the screen to disrupt your sleep and have an actual fatiguing effect then, no, its not common sense and, yes, you do need to hear and learn it from somewhere. If you don't have people around you educating you about these negative stimuli in our daily lives then there is good news... we have books!

The following books cover a range of tips, tricks, and dare I say it, 'hacks' that genuinely will improve your life just a little bit at a time. There are some great pointers on how to deal with tech in your life and how ROUTINE, an ultimate facilitator of personal development, can help you with getting to sleep at night and wake up well rested in the morning.

There are several books on sleep and rest alone. You spend around a third of your entire life asleep so it's worth paying it some attention. If you can improve your sleep then you are allowing your body an extra third of its entire life cycle to increase its efforts of physiological recovery AND allowing your mind enhanced psychological rest and recovery. The titles in this chapter have great advice on sleep performance and how to improve it. They look at technology avoidance late at night, behavioural patterns, post sleep routines, bedroom activity, bed sizes, sleep enhancing plants, bedroom decoration, light, sound, family interference and much more!

Outside of sleep, but within your house in general, you can also improve your surroundings to help improve yourself. Declutter all the shit out of your home and then don't fill it up again. Maintain a simple life with 'Ikegai' and give your life a kick up the arse with 'Get Your Shit Together'

Some of the books in here look at food consumption in general but there are no specific diet related books in here. And for good reason. There are a phenomenal amount of books on the market dealing with sensible eating suggestions, nominally a balanced a moderated diet, and then there are a load of books on popular, or fad, diets. This is a debate that you could write about forever and if you find dieting is something you're interested in then I implore you to go off and do your research rather than just buying the latest well marketed book (If you bought this book because it was well marked that is totally OK). The advice is always different depending on the source of the advice and that should be one of your primary concerns. Advice can be very much geared towards the sponsor of the research so make sure you know who paid for the latest 'advice' and how it may benefit them or their company.

Healthy living and a healthy lifestyle in general may add years to you life expectancy and moreover make those years enjoyable and palatable rather than a struggle where you carry an illness or degrading body and mind with you on the journey. It is no secret that western and eastern philosophies differ on lifestyles so instead of focusing on the differences between them may I suggest selectively picking the elements of both that work for you to improve your environment, body, headspace and surrounding relationships. Western medicine has far more of a reactionary focus on you when things go wrong and some eastern practices are more proactive, focusing on not letting things deteriorate in the first place. Brilliant! Use both. East can keep you healthy and west can fix you when something breaks. 'Ikigai' is a Japanese centric book that looks at how the healthy 100+ year olds there earn their 'Super Centennial' titles and how they enjoy their long lives. This is great but the book I would start with is 'The Four Pillar Plan'. This book blends a plethora of advice sources and makes them extremely practicable and actionable.

DO NOT MISS 'A Year of Living Danishly'. This has got to be one of the best self help books you'll ever read and the secret bonus is, it's not actually designed to be a self help book so there is ZERO element of preaching; rather just a ton of scientific proof told in a wonderful chronological narrative of an adventure story.

The one thing that all of the books have in common in this chapter is that they have divided all of their tips, advice and hacks into small, very actionable, pragmatic steps and so implementing just one small thing into your lifestyle, at a time is very manageable. The results may, in some cases be fairly instant, but in others you may need a little more time to realise their effects. Enjoy the instant results and have patience with the ones that require a bit of time to grow. You might not notice a small change or improvement but if you slowly add another small improvement and another one and another one the total resultant change will have a measurable and notable impact.

If you haven't read any of these books before then I envy you because the enjoyment of learning what is in them is amazing!

| | |
|---|---|
| The Four Pillar Plan | Rangan Chatergee |
| A Year of Living Danishly | Helen Russell |
| Get Your S**t Together | Sarah Knight |
| Ikegai | Hector Garcia |
| The Stress Solution | Rangan Chatergee |
| Minimalism | Ingrid Bjork |
| Sleep | Nick Littlehales |
| Rest | Alex Soojung |

The Four Pillar Plan - Dr Rangan Chaterjee

SCORE: 90%

OUTLINE: Great pragmatic advice from a medical professional.

REVIEW: Dr Chaterjee has some really fantastic and simple tips in this book that are easily adopted and well worth a listen to. They cover sections RELAX, EAT, MOVE SLEEP. All sections are worth a listen but, in particular, I like the advice on optimising sleep by avoiding screen time before bed and removing personal devices from your bedroom. There is a lot of science to back the negative affects of 'screen time' and this books advises on how to avoid those pitfalls as well as many, many more useful tips. The advice is solid and is packaged in a useful way so that you can immediately

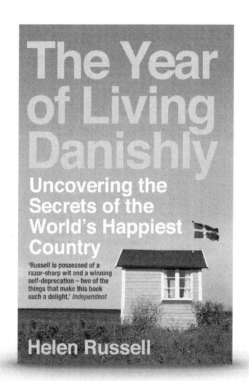

take action on any of his suggestions and implement it into your daily routine.

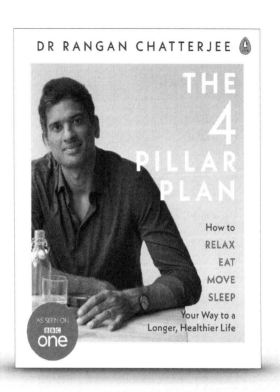

DR RANGAN CHATTERJEE

THE 4 PILLAR PLAN

How to
RELAX
EAT
MOVE
SLEEP

Your Way to a
Longer, Healthier Life

AS SEEN ON
BBC
one

# A Year Of Living Danishly - Helen Russell

SCORE: 100%

OUTLINE: Discovering why the danish are so happy.

REVIEW: So it turns out that the Danes have got this happy living seemingly licked. Shorter days at work, trust in the social state system, a willingness to pay loads of tax as they are confident with its use and many other reasons to be happy. They also seem to be sexually liberal in a controlled way within a very organised and rule based society. The author covers off examples of her Danish happiness research in an excellent narration of her trial year in Denmark. You get the trials, tribulations and even an evolving plot about the books featured characters, all in a factual book designed to allow you to take away some useful life lessons. This book is an ABSOLUTE MUST read! If this is the only book you ever read, and you follow some of the examples, your life will improve.

Bestselling
author of
*The Life-Changing
Magic of Not
Giving a F*ck*

# Get Your
# Sh!t Together

how *to* freak out less,
accomplish more,
*and* generally win *at* life

## Sarah Knight

# Get Your Sh!t Together - Sarah Knight

SCORE:81%

OUTLINE: A Self-Help Kick up the arse to encourage you to act.

REVIEW: From the author of the book 'How to not give a f*ck' comes this book which essentially tells you what a parent might tell you when trying to motivate you. Act, do something, sort your life out. Live a balanced and moderated life, take care of your physical and mental well being, keep your finances in check, don't worry about what others think and many more 'common sense' items of advice. It covers finance, health, happiness, pensions, houses, fitness etc. Nothing in this book is massively revolutionary and you may have heard it before but here it's delivered with a dose of motivation to boot. The title is obviously designed to be attention grabbing and the content is also the same. If you need a bit of a parental kick up the arse without the patronising bit then read away!

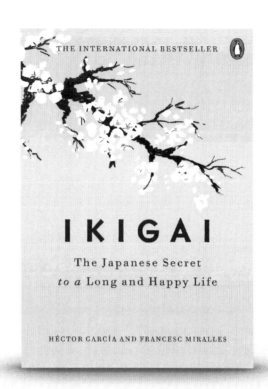

# IKIGAI

The Japanese Secret
*to a* Long and Happy Life

HÉCTOR GARCÍA AND FRANCESC MIRALLES

# Ikigai - Hector Garcia and Francesc Miralles

SCORE: 85%

OUTLINE: The Japanese secret to a long and happy life.

REVIEW: The author discusses her travels to Japan and searching out some of the world's oldest people to find out not only why they have sustained such high mileage but moreover why they are happy to live long and contented lives. There are essentially 6 key takeaways from the book that are expanded upon very well in each chapter. She highlights that the Japanese people observed stay active in body and mind and never retire. They take things slow and surround themselves with good friends

We all know you should keep in good shape and take care of your body but sometime it holds more gravitas when it comes from a cheerful super centennial. It's a relatively short book at 2.5hrs but it packs a lot of value and is a great complement or guide to other positive reading books.

The author of the bestselling *The 4 Pillar Plan*

DR RANGAN CHATTERJEE

# THE STRESS
# SOLUTION

IMPROVE YOUR HEALTH AND WELLBEING WITH MY EASY LIFESTYLE PLAN

THE **4**

STEPS TO A

**CALMER,**

**HAPPIER,**

**HEALTHIER**

YOU

# The Stress Solution - Dr Ragan Chatergee

SCORE: 82%

OUTLINE: An intellectual and pragmatic guide to stress reduction.

REVIEW: This is the second book I have read by Dr Ragan Chatergee and the format of this book follows that of the first, 'The Four Pillar Plan'. There are a several life hacks on how to reduce the stressors in everyday life that can often have an insidious build up leading to a chronic condition. The first solution is to discover the meaning of your life, your purpose to exists, this will result in mental fortitude, resistance to small stressors and an improved sense of well being. There is a little overlap in some of the first book's advice but it serves as a great revision of how to deal with new technologies, social media and sleep management, as well as many more topics, in a manner to reduce stress and improve quality of life. Eat well, exercise, give your phone a break and practice deliberate breathing.

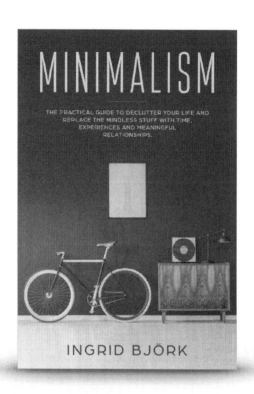

MINIMALISM

THE PRACTICAL GUIDE TO DECLUTTER YOUR LIFE AND
REPLACE THE MINDLESS STUFF WITH TIME,
EXPERIENCES AND MEANINGFUL
RELATIONSHIPS.

INGRID BJÖRK

# Minimalism - Ingrid Björk

SCORE: 75%

OUTLINE: Declutter, organise, clear up and think clearly. Please, you are preaching to the choir here!

REVIEW: The author covers off some basics about minimalism. She first starts by dispelling some myths about the movement of minimalism and what it doesn't involve. Then she applies some of the concepts to a practical scenario and illustrates the benefits. For instance decluttering your office and workspace is likely to help you declutter your mind and work more efficiently the tasks that are important for you to achieve. Apply this not only to being tidy physically but also try applying this to other areas of your life. Relationships, friendships, family, social media, financing, organisation etc etc. Clear out all the clutter and shit that you have to wade through and your life MIGHT become a whole lot easier.

**Nick Littlehales**

Elite sports sleep coach

# SLEEP

The Myth of 8 Hours,
the Power of Naps . . .
and the New Plan to
Recharge Your Body and Mind

# Sleep - Nick Littlehales

SCORE: 89%

OUTLINE: Sleeping tips, tricks and advice.

REVIEW: Nick discusses how a lot of societal and millennial technological changes are influencing and degrading our current sleep patterns and quality. There's standard advice about avoiding devices at night owing to the light they omit and some good post-bed and pre-bed routines. Tips on napping and sleep positions. The key take away for me is to measure sleep in 90min cycles and not just the amount of time you get. Aim for 5 x 90 min cycles a night and 35 a week. Recover missed cycles as soon as you can. Routine is key. Sex before sleep is also fine but you should, under his advice, post coital, go to separate beds for undisturbed recovery!

'This might be the book to finally persuade us that downtime isn't
in conflict with good work; rather, it's an essential ingredient of it'

OLIVER BURKEMAN
*Guardian* columnist and author of *The Antidote*

# Rest

## WHY YOU GET MORE DONE
## WHEN YOU WORK LESS

Alex Soojung-Kim Pang

# Rest - Alex Soojung

SCORE: 78%

OUTLINE: A day that starts well ends with rest that can be enjoyed without guilt. When you start early the rest you take is the rest you've earned.

REVIEW: This book talks about the importance of rest and how vital it has been in the attainment of success for CEOs, sports men and women, politicians etc etc. Obviously we all need rest but we need the right amount and it needs to be deliberate, sufficiently long in duration and qualitative. The author argues in favour of an early riser for productivity and has some great quotes throughout from prominent historical figures (I can't argue here as I've been compiling this book at 0530 everyday for a month). Quite a lot of the book is also based on productivity levels and on tips for creative people. One of the latter was to quit the day whilst you know what's next on the list. That way when you return to work the next day starting is done struggle free as you're not deciding, fresh, which direction to go in.

# 3. TIME MANAGEMENT.

*How to make the most of a limited resource.*

Ok. So one of the most common things you'll hear from someone who has exceptional time management is : "If you're too busy to look into time management then for that very reason you don't have have enough time to not look into it!" It's a bit smug really and easy to preach if you're all over your shit, but if you're behind and struggling to keep up then by definition, 'they' are correct. My top tip, as a recommendation to get started, would be to take a look at some of the following books when you're on holiday or at a time when you can allocate time to yourself. Start the book and as soon as you hear one thing that is applicable, stop! Then apply that one small thing. If you can make small incremental changes and implement them then the use of this whole book should be fairly manageable, especially if you read the 'Habits' chapter, and you manage to make some, or even just one, of the principles stick.

Whatever principles or changes you choose to adopt  also shouldn't take too long to introduce, remembering you're running low on time already, and you want to start seeing a small benefit. Then from here, hopefully you'll find it a positive reaffirming cycle whereby you gain a little more time and incrementally you introduce another time management concept. So you gain a little more free time and you invest some of that free time into learning about more methods to free up more time. This is the compounding effect in action and the reward is that eventually you'll be able to free capacity, allowing you to focus your spare time on something you choose to do rather than constantly chasing your tail and become exhausted. If you get into the finance sector of this book you will see this affect when dealing with personal debt as well. Often the hardest thing to do is to get started but once you have some momentum behind you you'll find it a lot easier to keep going!

Good and bad time management can also effect you health. Modern life produces many demands on our attention and drains the valuable resource of time from us ever single day. People try to ineffectively multi task and become overloaded with work, backed up job lists, notifications, commitments etc, etc and the list goes on and on and on. The management of your time, or non management of your time in some cases, can end up having an effect on your health. Your self esteem, work performance, stress levels and even your relationships can be adversely affected. Not You? Ok. How many times have you cancelled date night because you've had to work late or skipped a nutritious meal and replaced it with a dirty burger because you're in a rush? Or almost had a car accident because you just had to speed to make it to the airport on time? It's not just you, it's all of us. From presidents to porters and everything between.

The good news is that the reverse is true as well. Effective time management will help give you more clarity, more head space, less stress, maybe help with that insidiously increasing high blood pressure and obviously give you back more time. Im not saying that it is some miracle health cure, obviously not, but it can be a huge contributing factor to helping. Can good time management solve cancer? No. Can it help with diabetes? Maybe! If you had just another 10 spare mins a day would that give you the time to make a healthy packed lunch instead of using the takeaway option in your lunch break, then maybe it could. And that in turn that would save you some money as well. And in turn you'd then worry slightly less bout money and your stress would come down just a little. And if you add up all the benefits I bet fairly soon you'd see a total change that would make you healthier. All from a time management book! Who would have thought it.

There are less books in this chapter than some but the ones that are included are great! Brian Tracy is globally renowned for his expertise in the subject and for good reason. That's why he has multiple books in here and why his concepts have stood the test of time. Gary Keller's book, 'The One Thing' is also great and will have you changing your time management and prioritisation at the beginning of every day. Journalling can complement time management techniques nicely as the daily reminders of your most important thoughts and tasks help with prioritisation. Daily journalling is a habit that I have thankfully adopted and managed to maintain for years now. If you can journal it will help immeasurably with this topic.

Time is the one resource you can not get back. Ever. You can make money, loose money and you can make it all back again. The same is true for relationships and to a certain extent your health but you can not make time and you certainly can not get it back once it has gone. Protect your time and make the most of it. Do what you can to spend it efficiently and use it efficiently. Learn about how to manage it and how to optimise it.

A point I'll make here is that if you have time to listen to the news or to music on the way to work, whilst you work out or even when you are at work, then you also have time to change that habit into listening to a book on your commute. Audible is a life changer. I should have some kind of referral fee for the praises and recommendations I make for audible but I do not. It is no exaggeration to say that you can turn your phone into a library and a library that you use at that! The value you invest in spending time on learning and developing yourself will see returns, on that time invested, that you will reap positive changes and increased productivity from.

Just think, you'll be able to read/listen to all of these books when you would have previously had your attention consumed by bull shit news about a lying politician or singing the greatest hits of Backstreet boys. Back streets back alright!

Time Management      Brian Tracey
The One Thing      Gary Keller
Eat That Frog      Brian Tracey

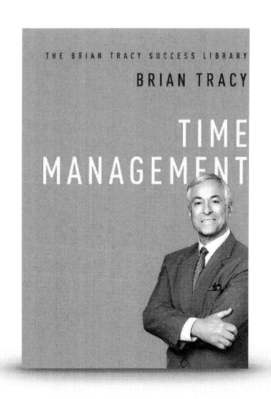

THE BRIAN TRACY SUCCESS LIBRARY

BRIAN TRACY

TIME
MANAGEMENT

# Time Management - Brian Tracy

SCORE:77%

OUTLINE: Great guide to time management.

REVIEW: Brian Tracy looks at tips and techniques to help manage your time including learning how and when to say NO, the 80/20 Principle to productivity and how to effectively start your day by "eating that frog" or "eating a whale one mouthful at a time". There are some fundamental principles in this book that are expanded in some of his further titles, but I would suggest starting here first. If you haven't read any time management books then this is going to blow your mind. If you are familiar with these types of self help books then this will, at the very least, be a great revision session.

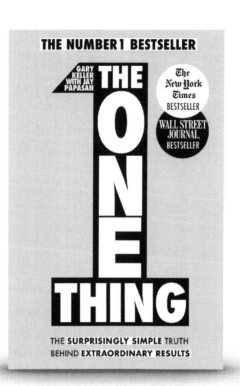

# The One Thing - Gary Keller, Jay Papasan

SCORE:99%

OUTLINE: Time management and prioritisation DONE!

REVIEW:This book is so good that the first thing I did when I finished it was to listen to it again from the beginning. It encompasses several key pieces of advice and rolls them all up into one book with one linking concept. The One Thing. Forget about the overwhelm of doing everything and just do one thing at a time. The author talks about having NOW GOALS where by you envisage your 'someday goal', way too big to achieve in a day, but then you figure out quickly what the 5 year goal would be to support the 'someday goal'. You then figure out the preceding 1 years goal, the 1 month goal, the 1 week goal and then the 1 day goal. Then you ask yourself 'What is the one thing that I could do RIGHT NOW to help that 1 day goal'? He has great practical tips to help achieve this like time blocking which is a great idea where you refuse to interact in anything that does not serve the purpose of that NOW GOAL for a total of 4 hours a day. Then you track how many days in a row you can do that. He also links it to Pareto's 80/20 law, The domino effect, which I won't ruin for you, and the difference between working hard at something and working at something with a purpose instead. I couldn't recommend this book enough and almost wish it was the first one that I had read!

# Eat That Frog - Brain Tracy.

SCORE: 79%

OUTLINE: Suck it up, Eat that fucking frog!

REVIEW: IN this book Brian Tracey looks at a really effective tool for prioritising your day and managing your time effectively. Eating the frog essentially refers to do the hardest and least desirable task first, marking it off as a win and then with a sense of satisfaction getting on with the rest of the day. In the rest of the day try adopting the illustrated principles such as the 80/20 rule to EVERYTHING, focus on key result areas, prepare thoroughly before you start, upgrade your skills and MANY MANY more!

There are so many really good strategies listed in this book that you really would benefit in actioning each chapter one at a time, or even selectively reading and actioning a chapter, rather than reading the book cover to cover and then trying to remember all the advice given! I'd even suggest making notes as you go through as a revision tool and a method of annotating exactly where you could apply the advice to. A great read.

# 4. MINDFULNESS & MENTAL HEALTH.

*Awareness of the mind and maintaining its health.*

Emotional and mental health is important because it's a vital part of your life and impacts your thoughts, behaviours and emotions. Being healthy emotionally can promote productivity and effectiveness in activities like work or school. It plays an important part in the health of your relationships, and allows you to adapt to changes in your life and cope with adversity.

This topic is always going to be sensitive and can feel like a minefield to write about as well. As of 2020 Mental Health is, thankfully, something that is losing its long held stigma and instead is something that can be openly discussed with friends, family and colleagues. If you are suffering from mental health issues yourself then my best advice is to seek professional help. I don't think a book is the magic elixir here. BUT if you know someone that has a mental health issue and you'd like to support them then reading about it and educating yourself is one of the best things you can do.

The younger, more naive and less educated version of me would have offered advice to a friend such as "cheer up mate, it's all in your head, just be happy" and then I would have, and I'm ashamed to write this, thought 'they are weak'. THAT IS WRONG !!!! If someone had a physical condition you would be mindful of it when interacting with them and a psychological one is just the same.

I am not saying that I am an expert on any of the subjects around mental health, far from it, but I have become more mindful after reading books about it. I now try to listen to friends rather than try to tell them what I would do all the time and offer solutions.

The books included in the below reviews are the ones that gave me some perspective on the matter. They will encourage you to be considerate and empathetic and that is a lot easier to fathom when you learn that some of the books are written by those that have suffered, and recovered, from mental health illnesses.

Don't take my word for it though. Here is a message from someone with Bipolar 2 Disorder: "Being mentally ill can be just a serious and debilitating as physical illness. However, physical illness can often be seen and more easily understood. There is still stigma associated with mental illness so it doesn't get discussed between the sufferer, friends or family. This must be overcome for healing to begin. It's also important to have a 'tool kit' to manage your mental health. Most of all be kind to yourself and don't be afraid to seek or recommend professional help. There is no shame in it. Often suffers will want to vent and offload, which is healthy, but are scared to do so"

Everyday there are small actionable steps that you can take, or encourage others to take, to improve your state of mental health. Small things like exercising, eating a balanced and healthy diet, opening up to other people in your life, taking a break when you need to, remembering something you are grateful for and getting a good night's sleep. All of these can be helpful in boosting your emotional health.

The books in this chapter really can help with gaining some insight to the factors that can contribute towards a healthy mind. journaling, avoiding stress, training your own brain, avoiding negativity, practicing gratitude and many, many more techniques. The titles that follow will also help you be mindful of others.

Proactively the books also deal with tips to keep the mind fresh and alert. They instil habits and concepts the keep you focusing on development and growth in the mind and staying active in both physical and psychological exercises.

Some parts of our modern society are moving in the right direction to help improve and support people with mental health concerns. Acceptance and openness in talking about the subject are being championed by people from everyday walks of life all the way through to political leaders and the monarchy. Mental health and wellbeing is also being dealt with in societies and industries, like the military, where it would have previously been labelled as a weakness or a 'lack of moral fibre'. These are positive trends but we need to be aware that around us we are surrounded by a culture of instant gratification and the need, especially in pop culture and media, to compare ourselves, our wares and possessions, or relationships and careers against others. The classic keeping up with the Joneses mindset that drives consumerism through comparison.

So whilst we are trying to be mindful of other peoples mental health, as well as monitoring and maintaining our own, we also need to be aware that there are things around us that potentially, constantly, oppose these efforts. When you realise that it is easy to be aware of it and in reading and learning more about it will help in that effort.

So lend and ear to a friend or reach out to someone who will help you off load. The following books are likely to partially help in advice but moreover they are likely to reassure someone that they are not alone their feelings and concerns. It may just be the antidote required to simply put their mind at rest.

| | |
|---|---|
| Positive Thinking | Napoleon Hill |
| The Practicing Mind | Thomas M Sterner |
| 13 Things Mentally Strong People Don't do | Amy Morin |
| Reasons to Stay Alive | Matt Haig |
| The Search For a Balanced Life | Sanjay Burman |
| TheBullet Journal Method | Ryder Carroll |

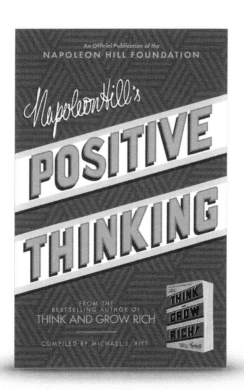

# Positive Thinking - Napoleon Hill

SCORE: 81%

OUTLINE: 10 Suggestions on how you might choose to act and react to maintain a positive outlook on life.

REVIEW: Essentially this book gives a load of tips and advice on how to instigate the power of a Positive Mental Attitude (PMA) every day. Clearly it's something we would all like to do but can't always manage. In each 10 minute chapter there are examples of how you could potentially adjust what you are currently practicing so as to have a more positive result than the ones you may be currently experiencing.

Taking possession of your own mind with conviction, keeping your mind on the things that you want and illuminating all negative thoughts by self inspection are all chapters the author discusses. I think the most pragmatic chapters were 'Set goals' and 'Study, Think and Plan Daily'. The reason for this is that they are physical, tangible things you can do with a mental health benefit.

DEVELOPING FOCUS & DISCIPLINE IN YOUR LIFE

The
# Practicing
# Mind

Master any skill or challenge
by learning to love the process

THOMAS M. STERNER

# The Practicing Mind - Thomas M Sterner

SCORE: 84%

OUTLINE: Don't beat yourself up so much. Life is a journey.

REVIEW: We are all going to die. It's the only thing really that everyone on this planet actually shares. Life is a journey and often over setting of goals can lead to a reduction in motivation. The author sets out that if we enjoyed the process of learning more and pushed back against the modern requirement for instant gratification and entitlement then we would all be a lot happier. One of the best analogies in the book is the story of a person swimming across the lake. If you kept your head out of the water the whole time, looking at where you were going, you would take longer to swim across. An efficient swimmer will take a few strokes, look up, adjust, work, monitor, adjust and so on. You just have to have faith sometimes that whilst you are working away at a goal you are progressing even if you're not getting the feedback and validation that you desire. Having goals is good, use them to help you steer on track like a rudder on a boat crossing the ocean. But don't cross the whole ocean cursing that you're not there yet. Just enjoy the actual aspect of sailing, the journey, chill and trust that you're moving in the right direction.

# 13

## Things
## Mentally
## Strong
## People
## **Don't** Do

Take back
your power,
embrace
change,
face your
fears &
train your
brain for
happiness
& success

The online
phenomenon
taking the
world by storm

**Amy
Morin**

# 13 Things Mentally Strong People Don't Do- Amy Morin

SCORE: 85%

OUTLINE: Own you power and train your brain.

A lot of sage advice will say "focus on what you want to achieve rather than what you want to avoid". This book does the opposite and just highlights what Amy Morin, the psychologist, advises her patients and herself, after a pretty harsh turn of events in her life, to do. This includes giving up self pity, it's a vicious circle, energy draining and unattractive (authors words, not mine). Don't give away your power by harbouring feelings of anger and resentment to others and don't shy away from change, step out of your comfort zone.

Don't give up after the first failure and don't expect immediate results. The biggest thing I learnt from this book was to try and make some time for yourself, by yourself. Some solitude away from the rest of the world and some time to just chill out - even when it seems almost uncomfortable to do so. And when you're working towards a big project don't expect to achieve the result in 5 mins. It takes time to achieve something that is great.

INTERNATIONAL BESTSELLER

Reasons
to Stay
Alive

"Brings a difficult and sensitive subject
out of the darkness and into the light." —Michael Palin

Matt Haig

MINDFULNESS & MENTAL HEALTH

# Reasons To Stay Alive - Matt Haig

SCORE: 84%

OUTLINE: An insight into the world unknown of a mental health sufferer/survivor.

REVIEW: This book offers some really good insights as to what people with depression, anxiety, panic attacks and other similar mental health issues go through. So if you're trying to learn about it to support a friend or you're going through it yourself and are learning then it has some great information. Some of it, particularly the suicidal discussions, can feel very raw to read but it's informative and I certainly feel like now I know what NOT to say to my friends that I probably would have said having not read this book. Well done Matt Haig for putting himself out there writing this book. That must have taken a lot of courage!

# The Search For A Balanced Life - Sanjay Burman etal

SCORE: 79%

OUTLINE: Views/opinions from some of the worlds leading experts on how to obtain and maintain a balanced life.

REVIEW: A gathering of top life coaches, spiritual leaders and medical professionals give their opinion on what constitutes a balanced life and how it can be maintained. One key message is that sometimes people strive for more success. That perceived success is often based on a comparison drawn between oneself and someone/something else. If you stop and think about what they have outside that one factor of success would you be prepared to swap your whole life for theirs? If not look at what success and balance you already have and appreciate that you are probably living a life that is congruent with your current values.

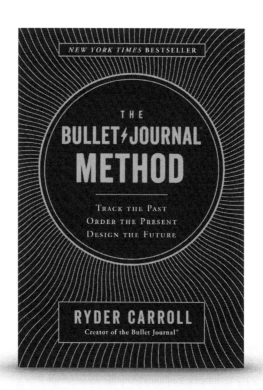

MINDFULNESS & MENTAL HEALTH

# The Bullet Journal Method - Ryder Carrol

SCORE:70%

OUTLINE: A different journaling methodology with a good attached pdf.

REVIEW: So, if you already journal, this book might add some ideas to your current repertoire. If you don't journal the book might seem more revolutionary. The advice seems sound and the method of bullet journaling seems to be a good idea. Some of the book can be a little confusing; for instance 'be flexible in your approach to how you journal but don't journal incorrectly and do it the way that's suggested', seems a bit contradictory to me. But I like how the author suggest breaking down daily journaling into different sections rather than monthly journalling and long term planning. I've adapted my own journal style after listening to several books, or parts of books, on the habit but I'll certainly be adopting a few of his tips. I won't however be buying a custom journal from them but rather use my current method of a ruled moleskin book. That is something the author is happy about though he mentions his journals as being available but doesn't ram it down your throat. Seems honest and genuine.

# 5. FINANCE & BUDGETING.

*Personal finance, budgeting and learning about money.*

This is probably one of the most valuable chapters in this book. Finances ARE really important but there are a lot of misconceptions, surrounding money, that put us off not only discussing the subject but wanting to learn about it and develop our understanding of the topic. 'The rich, 'the greedy' and 'money being the root of all evil' are just a few of these widely held opinions offered to you but have you ever spent much time considering why people have these opinions or why you may now have the same opinions yourself? Did you actually form them yourself, from experience, or were they perhaps handed down to you by older generations or from society as a whole? Either way we can not escape the fact, especially within something like an English culture, there is a taboo about about discussing financial matters. It seems vulgar to discuss your salary or even just the cost of something but really why should it? If you discuss your pay with someone else, and the result of the discussion is that you are comparatively being paid less, you may find that you subsequently seek a pay rise or to change your circumstances to earn or save more and then suddenly you are in a better position financially. So what's the problem? If you wanted to loose a little weight you'd probably have no issue discussing a food diet with someone to improve your situation. So if you have a friend who is financially healthier than you what is the problem with asking them about how they budget so that you can reallocate your resources and get in better financial shape?

Sorting out your finances might take a bit of effort but it will liberate you and free up a lot of capacity and resources. Money is not always about having more of it to spend but rather having enough of it to be free. That might be freedom from something as big as not committing suicide, shocking I know, but because of financial difficulty you would be surprised, or maybe not be surprised, at how frequently that sadly happens. Something more ubiquitous and closer to home will be arguing with your significant other about money, how often does that happen? Study after study reveals that couples and families argue most over finances. So learning to rectify your budgeting and financing are great places to start to alleviate some friction in the household.

A healthy financial situation will quite obviously reduce levels of stress personally and within your close relationships. So we can cite the development of financial knowledge as being a good idea for healthy relationships. It is then not difficult to see how wealth development can lead to other areas of health development. Reduced stress and anxiety help mental health whilst the ability to afford health care or elective health care and the freedom to purchase healthy food choices all contribute to physiological health.

Sorting out your finances IS NOT HARD. I promise you that. When I was 18 I got my first credit card and my actual thoughts, as I sat down to spend the money at the time, were 'FREE MONEY'! I did not heed any of the advice given to me and instead went off to learn the mistakes my own way and over the next 10 years ended up with multiple cards and just under £20k in debt. Maybe you need to go off and learn those mistake yourself or hopefully you're better at taking advice than I am?

The books in this chapter WILL change your life and help free you from financial constraints. I would implore you to read all of them but if you only read one then you MUST read Rich Dad Poor Dad. In fact this is the most important book I have ever read. Full stop! That book is at the beginning of the chapter because I feel it is the most valuable one to read first, even before learning how to set yourself an effective budget. It has a concept in it that will fundamentally change the way you look at money and how you spend it and knowing that principe will then set you in good strength to action other concepts in other titles.

Because money is such a vast topic I have included a book for all levels and what I hope you'll find is if you do decide to progress through the books you'll slowly develop your understanding and education. The books develop in levels of detail, complexity and theory and as you progress through this will pair your level of understanding. Of course if you already have a grasp of some of the basics you'll probably find more value and development toward the middle and the end of the chapter. So once you have read 'Rich Dad, Poor Dad' you can then look at personal finances. How to essentially get out of debt, how to save and invest a little and how to prepare for your future. If you go all the way through the books in the chapter you'll learn how some of the globes wealthiest families preserve their wealth over generations, why some of the richest individuals in the world end up dedicating their lives to philanthropy and what investments stand the test of time through a vast array of challenges.

Money will buy you stuff but eventually, if you can get out of the consumer mindset, more money will, most importantly, buy you another far more precious commodity; TIME. If you have money you will eventually have the freedom of time and that is the biggest life lesson I have ever learnt. Time freedom is real wealth. Wealth is not a high figure in your bank account. Being wealthy is being on top of your finances and subsequently not worrying about where your next mortgage payment is coming from, not worrying if you lose your job or go through a global recession, and not having to give all your time to a company in exchange for money.

Don't spend your life being a prisoner to your pay cheque and waiting for retirement. Get on top of your financial shit, be positive and proactive about it. Work toward and then enjoy time freedom.

| | |
|---|---|
| Rich Dad Poor Dad | Robert Kiyosaki |
| How to be Smart with Money | Duncan Banytyne |
| I Will Teach You To Be Rich | Ramit Sethi |
| The Compound Effect | Darren Hardy |
| Wealth Secrets of the 1% | Sam Wilkin |
| The Automatic Millionaire | David Bach |
| Money | Rob Moore |
| The Ascent of Money | Niall Ferguson |

# Rich Dad Poor Dad - Robert Kiyosaki.

SCORE: 100%

OUTLINE: GAME CHANGING book that will revolutionise your entire life.

REVIEW: This book WILL change your life. Especially if you're not rich! Who knew that your house wasn't actually your biggest asset? No, me neither! It is this simple: an asset is something that puts money in your pocket and a liability does the opposite; it takes it out. So what? Well Robert Kiyosaki illustrates in this book that he had 2 dads, kind of, one that was rich and one that was poor, and he learnt that you NEED assets in your life, not liabilities. This in itself sounds harsh but it isn't it's just matter of fact and in the book you will learn how a few simple changes can really turn your life around. You will learn what Roberts Rich Dad and Poor Dad taught him, their differing opinions, and how, if you want to be wealthy, you need to start making your money work for you rather than you working for your money.

To my younger self I would say: If there is only one book you could read for the rest of your life it is this one. READ IT!! RIGHT NOW!!

The sequel to this book is Cashflow Quadrant by Robert Kiyosaki. Another epic book that will help you alter your future finances for the better (Scored at 93%). But it really must be read after the first book reviewed here.

DUNCAN BANNATYNE

HOW TO BE
SMART
WITH YOUR
MON£Y

Up-to-the-Minute
Advice from
the Star of
Dragons' Den

# How To Be Smart With Your Money - Duncan Bannatyne

SCORE: 88%

OUTLINE: Some common sense money chat.

REVIEW: In this book Bannatyne imparts some common sense money tips. This is great for introducing some sound fundamentals about how to budget, how to save money and how to make more money. In brief he wants you to keep more than you spend and offers advice on how you can increase that gap. Also if you spend more than you make he will offer helpful advice on how to close that gap!

The New York Times and Wall Street Journal bestseller

I WILL TEACH YOU TO BE RICH

*by*
RAMIT SETHI

*founder and writer of*
iwillteachyoutoberich.com

No Guilt.
No Excuses.
Just a
6-Week
Programme
That Works

# I Will Teach You To Be Rich  - Ramit Stehi

SCORE: 85%

OUTLINE: A 6-week schedule to sort out your finances.

REVIEW: In this book the author does actually have some really sound advice on how to work toward s 'Making You Rich'. It is easy to judge a book on its cover and in this case I underestimated this book. For some one just starting into financial improvement his strategies are sound.

How to pay down debt, how to save, some basics on waisting and money mindset are all in here. The 6-week plan initially sounds far fetched but the aim is not to make you Rich in that time frame. It's a 6 week pragmatic work schedule and action plan for you to follow and get you on track.

The author and I would probably disagree on budgeting but thats a personal thing so listen to what he says and see what you think yourself. An informative and humorous read. Yes, the book is American centric but the tips, tricks and advice are all transferable. Also some great suggestions of extra blogs and further reading.

"A real program, with real tools that can change your life and make your dreams a reality."
—DAVID BACH, bestselling author of *The Automatic Millionaire*

# THE
# COMPOUND
# EFFECT

*New York Times, Wall Street Journal, and USA Today Bestseller!*

## JUMPSTART
## YOUR INCOME, YOUR LIFE,
## YOUR SUCCESS

# DARREN HARDY

Publisher of *SUCCESS* magazine

# The Compound Effect - Darren Hardy

SCORTE: 99%

OUTLINE: A game changing way to make future decisions.

REVIEW: The heart of this book is the theory of compounding. Essentially by actioning small but positive decisions, each day, consistently over time, you will yield positive results. This is applied to different categories. Financially the author looks at how saving a small amount of money, ie; for a pension, early on in life will deliver compounded results. The money you save grows with a small return, that return plus the original money grows and then gets added to the next set of savings. Then that whole pot grows. And on, and on, and on. You get the picture. He also looks at healthy choice decisions in eating and highlights that it does only take a few small things to steer you in the right direction. It's a fascinating book as it actually gives you pragmatic tips to implement.

When you grasp the concept it will have a profound effect on how you consider a lot of you decisions. It highlights as many books do though that you need to be consistent and take action! Read it now and implement it.

# Wealth Secrets
# of the 1%

## THE TRUTH ABOUT
## MONEY, MARKETS AND
## MULTI-MILLIONAIRES

# Sam Wilkin

# Wealth Secrets Of The 1% - Sam Wilkin

SCORE: 79%

OUTLINE: Documentary on Money and wealth strategies.

REVIEW: Some really detailed, if not a little long at times, accounts of some of the wealth strategies and secrets of the global super rich. This is not really a 'how-to' guide but more of a documentary. The style of the narration and writing is informative and at times humorously sarcastic. It is fairly up to date, as of 2020, and covers Ancient Romans all the way through to social media kings. A GREAT chapter, finally giving me a comprehendible understanding of why the 2008 world financial crisis happened and why, when you think the banks would suffer, they didn't because they were 'to big to fail' and thus were rescued. The last chapter looks at some familiar personality traits of the super wealthy and without recommending it 'suggests' if you elect similar traits you will be in with a better chance of emulating their wealth. It's like a long but interesting documentary rather than a self help book to be honest.

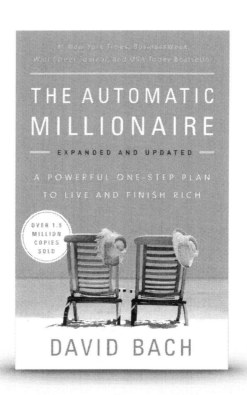

# The Automatic Millionaire  - David Bach

SCORE: 88%

OUTLINE: Make some small adjustments to your spending habits to ensure that you can retire rich.

REVIEW: If you have already heard of the concept of 'paying yourself first' then this book will reaffirm that message/belief and if you haven't then this concept is an excellent one to get started on. Trust me, I do it. The message is simple. Apply the 'latte factor' and save a small percentage of your income before you pay any other bills. Start with 1% of your salary and put it aside on pay day. Eventually you will, over time increase that percentage to as much as 20%. Some of the numbers on this are staggering and if you put that aside and invest it wisely it will reap HUGE benefits when you're at retirement age. The 'latte factor' is where you cut out 2 of your 5 lattes per day and save £10 a day. Invest it annually and after 30 years your money pot is in the region of £350-450,000.00 !!!!!! So that latte you drink doesn't cost £2.90 now, it costs you nearly £0.5m in 30 years.

# Money - Rob Moore

SCORE: 90%

OUTLINE: LOADS of information on how to 'Know More, Make More and Give More' by Rob Moore.

REVIEW: This is a really in depth look into money. A multi faceted approach including the history and future of money, the psychology around it and what it means to live with or without it. There are quite a few links and cross references to other people's theories. What I would say is, for instance, the author will briefly discuss 80/20 principle - where another author may cover that single topic in an entire book. So there is a lot of information but readers may have to dive even further into other books to pick up the full story of some topics. It's a long book but a very interesting one and one I would add to a list of life time 'must reads' if you are at all concerned with furthering yourself financially in life.

If you like this book the you'll love 'Life Leverage' by the same author to help with life in general.

Niall Ferguson

'The most brilliant historian of his generation' THE TIMES

The Ascent of

MONEY

A Financial History of the World

'Dazzling ... extraordinarily timely' SPECTATOR

# The Ascent Of Money- Niall Ferguson

SCORE: 77%

OUTLINE: A look at global economy and the results of bad banking decisions.

REVIEW: The Ascent of money is really quite an interesting book. It's not the place to start if you're looking at some budgeting help, not at all. But. If you want a better understanding of he financial world then this book is full of content. The author looks at the history of money, some of the huge errors made by banks, where insurance started, and most importantly just how fallible we humans are.

I think this book will give you a broader aspect of finance and economy and how all the big pieces fit together to influence you. If you can understand and pay attention to what is going on around you and in the wider world you will probably have a better chance of being able to make valuable and informed decisions about what to do with your money.

# 6. COMMUNICATION & RELATIONSHIPS.

*Build, maintain & get more from our human interactions.*

Relationships and communicating within them are everywhere around us. We maintain important and life enhancing relationships with family, friends, romantic partners, work colleagues and we maintain benign relationships with people we connect with everyday. I don't think the importance of relationships can be overstated. humans are very social creatures and a lot of our highest needs are fulfilled on a psychological level; dependant on meaningful relationships and effective communication.

Maslow's hierarchy of needs is an extremely well established and accepted model of human aspiration that highlights at it bottom and basic levels the human need for survival with food, shelter and reproduction. As you progress from basic needs to the pinnacle levels needs you pass through a stage of love and belonging before hitting the top with esteem and self actualisation. All the levels contain elements of belonging to a group, acceptance, respect, friendship, family and intimacy. Extroverted or introverted it doesn't matter. Whichever classification you identify with, or partially identify with, we all have an innate desire to fit into some type of group, develop, nurture and importantly maintain relationships.

Now maintaining these relationships can be almost as difficult, if not harder, than developing them in the first place. Everyone has seen some form of relationship end that they didn't want to give up and it can normally be attributed to a level of communication.

You'll find in this chapter that the scores are probably disproportionately higher than in any other chapter. I have no background in human behavioural psychology or relationship management. I do however find it fascinating how an author can articulate an obvious reason, obvious only once you know the answer, as to why a situation you were involved in panned out the way it did and why, after it all happened, you left scratching your head searching for the answers as to what just happened.

Imagine you've just had a huge argument with a family member, a work colleague, a friend or a romantic partner (or combination of the above). The dust has settled and you feel like you haven't really reached a conclusion, that you don't know what started or why it was so important but what you do know is that no one is satisfied with the outcome and you might have to return back to the status quo with all the upset and anger not really achieving anything. Well in the following titles you'll get a HUGE amount of insight as to why it may have happened, who acts in certain types of ways and most importantly how you and 'they' can probably deal with it far better in the future.

Humans are all very different. We have different backgrounds, different beliefs, different aspirations, different languages and different personality traits. There are a lot of variable that affect us and at the moment there are over seven billion people, who we share this planet with, who we might have to interact with. There is not a 'one size fits all' way of interacting with people but there are some concepts and theories discussed in the following books that can help when trying to foster a meaningful relationship with anyone.

I think one of the important things to realise when you read these books is that they are not trying to teach you the correct way to talk to someone or how to influence someone. They are however offering you some insight to other techniques that you may not have already tried and if you're seeking out these titles it might also mean it's not because there is a problem that you are trying to fix but perhaps also that you have a good relationship, and communicate well with someone, and you want that experience to remain positive.

Take for instance 'The 5 Love Languages'. Yes the book was designed to rescue marriages but if you have a good relationship and read it then you will have more tools to keep things running smoothly. Rescuing a relationship will be hard work, maintaining a good one will be comparatively easy.

Relationships involve more that one person. Some relationships, like that you have with teams of co workers, bosses, children, parents, spouses and friends, will sometimes have many different people, and personality types, within them. If you want to try and gently influence some of these people, rather than deceptively coerce them then you'll find loads of the book reviews, and subsequently the books themselves, really useful.

Psychology, behavioural theory and human economics can offer a fascinating insight to how other people tick. Realising that you are not always right, and that everyone else around you are not complete idiots, will develop your compassion for understanding and develop your inclination to just listen. And it's surprising what you will hear and learn when you allow others the freedom to share what's on their mind.

Some of these books are the most interesting books I have ever read. What's more a lot of the authors have a number of books so if you find yourself gripped by their writing you can always explore that authors other work further.

| | |
|---|---|
| The Five Love Languages | Gary Chapman |
| The School of Life | Alain De Botton |
| Talking to Strangers | Malcom Gladwell |
| The Chimp Paradox | Steve Peters |
| The book you wish your parents.. | Philippa Perry |
| How To Win Friends and Influence People | Dale Carnige |
| Surrounded by Idiots | Thomas Erikson |

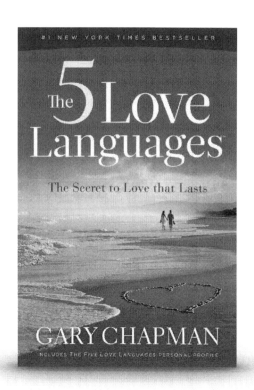

# The 5 Love Languages - Gary Chapman

SCORE: 99%

OUTLINE: Communication game changer!

REVIEW:There are, according to this author 5 love languages. Words of Affirmation, Acts of Service, Touch, Gifts and Quality Time. Like it or not you will find that you fit into some or all of these categories and the benefit of the book is HUGE. Whether you are rescuing a relationship that is on the brink of divorce or you are trying to identify why you don't get on well with someone at work, you will certainly gain an advantage from reading this book. As a newlywed the book is a great way of identifying your behaviours and discussing why you prefer certain displays of affection.

I would recommend this book, and the further titles in the series of 'Love Language' books to anyone that is working on a relationship, be it romantic or professional, anywhere in their lives. So basically that is everyone. In fact this book is so good that I now give it as a gift to every couple that I know that are getting married.

# THE
# SCHOOL
# OF LIFE

## AN EMOTIONAL EDUCATION

*Introduced by*
## ALAIN DE BOTTON

# The School Of Life - Alain de Botton and Hallie Anson

SCORE: 90 %

OUTLINE: AMAZING.

REVIEW: In this book the author looks at some of the psychology behind behavioural traits that we experience within our relationships. It gives a lot of insight as to why we act the way we do during certain situations of passion, infidelity, rage, anger and more. This is one of the only books that I have listened to again immediately after it has finished. The reason for this is that I wanted to re-digest the information because it was of such a value.

# Talking
## to
# Strangers

WHAT
WE SHOULD
KNOW ABOUT
THE PEOPLE
WE DON'T
KNOW

# Malcolm
# Gladwell

#1 *NEW YORK TIMES* bestselling author of *OUTLIERS*
and host of the podcast *REVISIONIST HISTORY*

# Talking To Strangers - Malcom Gladwell

SCORE: 90%

OUTLINE: Why we are so bad at talking to strangers?

REVIEW: Why are humans so bad at interacting with people they don't know? Well this book covers cultural biases, systemic errors that are latent in industries and establishments and micro and macro level psychology that cause people to make mistakes. The book rotates around the account of a black woman who commits suicide in police custody after being arrested for a traffic offence. Shocking, yes, but understandable? Well it will be when you read the book. Another fascinating book by Malcom Gladwell and a very, very worthy read.

# The Chimp Paradox - Steve Peters

SCORE: 91%

OUTLINE:  About to react? Box that Chimp!

REVIEW: Box that chimp! This book is a great insight into human behaviour and for some of the stimuli that have evolved our personalities. That author leans into the theory that you can change your behaviour, your overt actions, but not your personality and your inner thoughts. He also looks at which parts of the brain cause certain primal thoughts verses those that involve educated reasoning. This book will certainly help you identify what drives your sometimes uncontrollable behaviour. The book helps give you a common language to discuss behaviour with others so that the next time you find yourself reacting to a situation you may find yourself using the authors advice; acknowledge the chimp, then box it!

# The Book You Wish Your Parents Had Read

(and Your Children Will be Glad That You Did)

Hugely warm, wise, hopeful and encouraging
Alain de Botton

## Philippa Perry

# The Book You Wish Your Parents Had Read - Philippa Perry

SCORE: 80%

OUTLINE: Great parenting advice and education.

REVIEW: This book is written with a very interesting perspective of what you would want your parents to have perhaps read. It's also good to read if you are thinking of having children or indeed if you have children up to a teenage or early adult age. There are some good communication advice tips on trying to deal with trauma and conflict resolution whereby the author recommends looking at the objective from the child's point of view. This book is probably worth a read every 3 to 4 years as a revision aid to remind you of some of the concepts that the author discusses, including attachment and detachment theory, and also as a reminder of how to manage certain tantrum style situations.

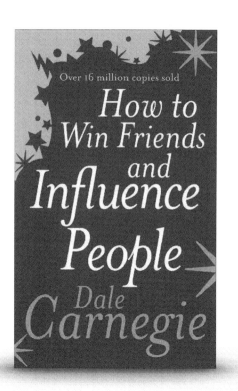

Over 16 million copies sold

# How to
# Win Friends
# and
# Influence
# People

### Dale
### Carnegie

# How To Win Friends & Influence People - Dale Carnegie

SCORE: 83%

OUTLINE: Need to get your point across??? Try this book.

REVIEW: A lot of examples of practical applications of behaviour and consideration that help to influence people and earn their acceptance. Less deceptive and more genuine than I had anticipated. Useful, friendly and achievable advice that helps you gain acceptance in a genuine manner. I think one of the important things to note is that the persuasive or influential techniques that you can adopt in this book seem to be perfectly fine as long as you are both well intentioned and genuine in your cause. In the wrong hands these techniques could be almost weaponised by the likes of a con man or illegitimate influencer. If nothing else when you've finished reading this book you may find alternative ways of articulating your opinion where you have previously failed despite considering it very important such as in conflict resolution scenario.

# surrounded by idiots

**The Four Types of Human Behavior**
and How to Effectively Communicate
with Each in Business (and in Life)

• • • •

# thomas erikson

# Surrounded By Idiots - Thomas Erikson

SCORE: 82%

OUTLINE: Why is everyone, except me an idiot?

REVIEW: Ha. I think a lot of people can agree at some point that they have felt everyone around them is an idiot. But the truth of the matter is we are all just different humans. The author looks at the red, blue, yellow and green classification of human psychology and behaviour and how we all tend to identify with some of the classifications. It's not that we are one or the other but more often than not a blend of a few colours. The author highlights behaviours indicative of the classifications and then highlights why they may not exactly get on. The key takeaway for me in the book is that a successful team is made up of a blend of the colours. In an organisation you need some people that are visionaries, some that are detailed workers, some risk takers, some logical thinkers and some cautious socialites. The knack is finding a good leader to merge these traits and keep the peace!

# 7. INSPIRATION.

*Some of the worlds greatest people illustrated.*

Is inspiration hard to come by? No, I don't think so but I would argue that some of the inspiration that is available in the mass media is utter dog shit and won't do anyone any good. Now let's discuss Mr Average, or Miss, or Mrs, or Ms, and assume they live an average life. They probably come home after an average job, where they watch the clock all day, they eat some average food and then they join the rest of the nation and watch average, over dramatised, sensational TV and are inspired by what they see. Or they are inspired by what is around them. It's a commonly used phrase that 'you are the sum total of the five people you most often surround yourself with'. If one of those people has been replaced by a TV then Average Joe can only hope to become a minor, 15min, celebrity on a reality TV show, and this is probably their ultimate hope, or be the partner to someone who is rich and will look after them or ALARMINGLY, in this day in age can live lavishly when they inherit their parents money. Well good fucking luck Average Joe because the chance of being on a tripe TV show and becoming famous are slim and its not a healthy way through life either. Finding a footballer to marry is going to be very slim and if you manage to find one how do you plan on attracting them being Ms Average? Finally the inheritance saga. Average Joes Parents, if they are reasonably well off and in good health, might live until they're 90 maybe 100 maybe 110? And that makes them 60, 70, 80 years old by the time they get their hands on their decreasing wealth. Good luck Joe. Enjoy being Average forever.

I don't think that's you and if you're looking to inspire someone else, who is like Joe, then there is a far better way of doing it. And if you think you want to inspire someone beyond their current level then there are a whole hosts of books, biographies and autobiographies you can read or listen to. These come with a warning though. Some peoples memoirs are utter garbage. I have had the displeasure of listening to them and I have omitted them from the reviews. You're welcome.

There are some mind blowing books coming up in this chapter though and I would easily say that the first one is the best. I've given it the highest mark because it belongs in my top 10 books of all time and it is buy a guy who can inspire anyone to do more, achieve more, work harder, work longer and not only that but he will also question why you are doing it all in the first place.

David Goggins wrote 'You Can't Hurt Me' and rejected publishing deals to publish it himself. This guy is an absolute machine. If Average Joe wanted to be the best footballer in her class then you may assumed a driven version of her would want to be the best in the school, or the state. Give her this book, ignore the expletives, and she'll want to be the US Women's World Cup Football Captain. Goggins' journey is remarkable. He is so inspirational that I used this book to help inspire a friend of mine to fight like a mother fucker. That friend of mine went to hospital with a stomach ache and came out with stage four cancer diagnosis. Now we all, probably, know someone affected by cancer. They are normally going to be cancer victims or cancer survivors. And it is the mentality of the survivor that an inspirational book can help you have rather than the victim. That friend of mine is currently fighting a phenomenal fight. I gave her Goggins' book and said that if she wanted I would replicate his line of support to her rather than pussy foot around her. Right now she is fighting well and surpassed the doctors odds already. Oh and when she's not fighting cancer she's helping edit this book just because. The editor of this book is a fighter but if you know someone who is curling up like a victim give them a little helping hand in their fight. Give them some inspiration that will occasionally light the fire inside them that gives them that ounce of energy to get up and climb a mountain on the day that everyone else in their position would be cowering away.

Inspiration comes in many forms and from many people. There are some rags to riches stories in here as well as the prominent stories of world famous figures such as Michelle and Barack Obama. In fact, both of their autobiographies are in here and Michelle's is first because I actually think, for inspiration, you'll get slightly more from it, though both are great reads.

Perspective is one of the things that I think a lot of people seem to lack. Again I doubt this is you because people who are open minded often seek out, or are given these types of books. But there are stories that can give you perspective if you have not had the chance to experience the events themselves. A recent example of this can be seen in the Pandemic that was Coronavirus or COVID

19. A younger generation described this as 'our version of the World War'. Please! You must be fucking joking?!?! A war is where you risk your life to save the lives or territories of other peoples' and where you regularly deal with the mental prospect that you may die today for someone else's benefit. During the pandemic people were being asked to 'stay at home'. That is it. Stay in your warm comfortable house, do nothing and the government will also give you money. Massive lack of perspective. Give them the book '81 Days below Zero' and they might have an idea of hardship. A pilot, not actually at war but delivering aircraft, who crashes and as a lone survivor must get out of the icy, snowy tundra of Alaska.

So give someone, or yourself, some supporting inspiration, some perspective inspiration or just highlight what can be done by people who aren't necessarily special but typically just work hard, are consistent, determined, disciplined and put in some grit.

| | |
|---|---|
| Can't Hurt Me | David Goggings |
| The Greatest | Matthew Syed |
| Steve Jobs | Walter Isacson |
| Becoming | Michelle Obama |
| Total Recall | A. Schwarzenegger |
| Empire | Howard Hughes |
| The Audacity of Hope | Barack Obama |
| Winning | Alistair Campbell |

CAN'T HURT ME

MASTER YOUR MIND AND DEFY THE ODDS

DAVID GOGGINS

NEW YORK TIMES BESTSELLER

# Can't Hurt Me - David Goggins

SCORE: 100%

OUTLINE: An uncommon man amongst uncommon men; a warrior.

REVIEW: Goggings tells his phenomenal story via an audio book/ podcast that has eleven chapters of mind blowing resilience, fortitude, courage, persistence and mental toughness. If you need any inspiration to push harder at your task, to persist longer with your failures or go for your lofty goals, then look no further. I have never come across an account of anyone as tough and hard as this man. Whilst each chapter focuses on one of his triumphs over adversity he continually points out that he is not the hero, the reader is the hero. He highlights all that he has been through, one draw dropping chapter after another, in an effort to illustrate that the mind is your biggest strength and your biggest weakness. He encourages you to 'callus your mind' , 'take souls' and in the end, perhaps most importantly to take care of your body especially if you have spent years abusing it ! This guy is so mentally tough that this book is essential reading for anyone going through a rough spot!

# The Greatest - Matthew Syed

SCORE: 92%

OUTLINE: Why Sport is not just sport and what the greatest achievers can impart on us all.

REVIEW: Matthew Syed has another really interesting book focusing mainly around competitive sport and how there are many transferable traits that athletes exhibit; traits that we would all do well to emulate. There are a load of really interesting case studies that have a lessons contained within them. A little bit of overlap from other books but only a small percentage. Insightful and informative read that may not change your life but that will probably change your opinion.

Syed is an incredible author and if this book interests you I can recommend Black Box Thinking, Bounce and Rebel Ideas. All of these will open your mind.

Steve Jobs by Walter Isaacson

© Albert Watson

# Steve Jobs - Walter Isaacson

SCORE: 85%

OUTLINE: Steve Jobs from start to shut down.

REVIEW: This is a long book. 25hrs. The narrator, on the audio version, is a little slow but double the speed and it's still an easy read. It's a good biography covering everything from the early back ground of Jobs and his ancestors through to his death. It's an inspirational read to see how an adopted child came from a working class background to become one of the modern worlds most revolutionary and entrepreneurial men. There are some revealing insights into his professional and personal relationships. An inspiring read, if a little long. It's a bit like all the 'Jobs' films in one with A LOT more detail.

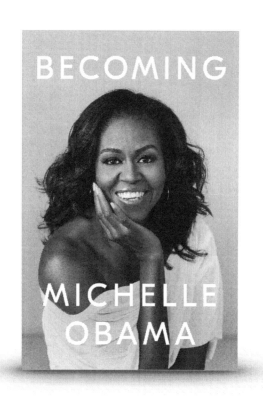

# Becoming - Michelle Obama

SCORE: 93%

OUTLINE: A synopsis of the life of the former First Lady.

REVIEW: In this book Michelle Obama narrates the story of her own life from her youth through to the present day. There are some fantastic insights into the private lives of one of the World's most powerful couples and it is amazing to see the huge contrast between some of the autobiographies from other presidents. Michelle Obama is more than a president's wife though. Much more. She was actually Barack's legal mentor in his first job and I've no doubt there are countless times when she has guided him, rather than the opposite, which I'm sure is regularly assumed. There are some heart warming and heart wrenching stories from this powerful woman who is a strong advocate for minority and women rights.

# Total Recall - Arnold Schwarzenegger

SCORE: 90%

OUTLINE: Arnie's amazing autobiography.

REVIEW: Wow.  A ton of things I never new about The Terminator. I don't think it matters if you don't like this guy, you don't have to, but you can not help but admire his persistence, determination and ambition. He's not a perfect citizen, he will be the first to admit it, but his story of Austrian rags to Californian riches is iconic. The book is entertaining for sure and if you think someone needs some inspiration for determination or a reality check on their first world problems then suggest this as a read. I'd love to sit down and ask this guy a million questions. What a legend.

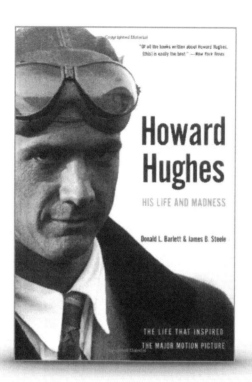

"Of all the books written about Howard Hughes, [this] is easily the best." —New York Times

# Howard Hughes

HIS LIFE AND MADNESS

Donald L. Barlett & James B. Steele

THE LIFE THAT INSPIRED
THE MAJOR MOTION PICTURE

# Empire  -Donald Bartlett and James Steele

SCORE: 80%

OUTLINE: The mind blowing history of an ego-centric American icon.

REVIEW: After reading 'Ego is the enemy' by Ryan Holiday this book was recommended to me by audible. It's not surprising as many of the lessons and points in that book are pointed out in Howard Hughes' Life. This book does though contain some remarkable insights into the man's life and how he battled against mental health issues in his daily pursuit of greatness, even if it was fuelled by ego and financed by his inherited wealth. There are some incredible elements of iconic motivation and examples of a man who was committed, driven, unique and incredibly ambitious.

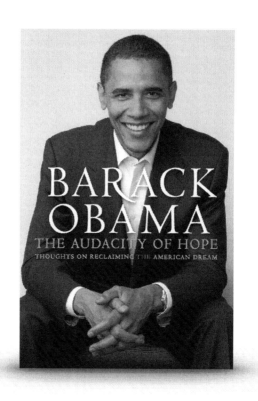

# The Audacity Of Hope - Barak Obama

SCORE: 82%

OUTLINE: Obama's recommendations on improving US politics.

REVIEW: This book, which is also read by Obama, covers some amazing insights into how US politics works. It looks at the concerns affecting it, like the integration of big money donations, reliance on media, and also how one of the biggest concerns amongst voters is that elected Senators will become corrupted by Washington. It also looks at the honest side of politics, what some are trying to achieve and how money can be a hugely limiting factor in most cases. That said, multi millionaire candidates can still loose to the underdogs if the message of sincerity is transmitted and received effectively. There are also more personable accounts of his marital and parental relationships whilst in politics.

BILL GATES
JACK WELCH
BARACK OBAMA
TANNI GREY-THOMPSON
ANNA WINTOUR
JEFF BEZOS • MICHAEL GORBACHEV • ELON MUSK
WARREN BUFFETT • NICK FALDO
CLASS OF '92 • NADIA COMANECI • ADE ADEPITAN
MERCEDES F1 • DAVE BRAILSFORD
JOSE MOURINHO
LAYNE BEACHLEY • TIGER WOODS
FLOYD MAYWEATHER
BEN AINSLIE • ANDY McCANN
ANGELA MERKEL
JOHN BROWNE • BONO • MATTHEW BENHAM
RICHARD BRANSON

## ALASTAIR CAMPBELL

# WINNERS

# AND HOW THEY SUCCEED

NELSON MANDELA
CHARLES DUNSTONE • MARTHA LANE FOX
STEVE JOBS • JUSTIN KING • BRIAN LARA
HAILE GEBRSELASSIE
BILL CLINTON • SHANE WARNE
JIMMY WALES • MICHAEL PHELPS
ARIANNA HUFFINGTON
SAM TRICKETT • SACHIN TENDULKAR
NARENDRA MODI
REF CHARDSOLL • EDDIE JONES + MICHAEL JORDAN
SAM WARBURTON • JOE TORRE
DIEGO MARADONA • EDI RAMA
GARRY KASPAROV
JIM O'NEILL • BRIAN O'DRISCOLL
LIONEL MESSI • KEVIN STACEY • LARRY PAGE
ALEX FERGUSON • SEB COE
LEIGH MATTHEWS • GARY LINEKER
PETE CARROLL • TOM BRADY • STEVE PETERS • WILLIE WALSH
DAVID BECKHAM • HILLARY CLINTON • JONNY WILKINSON
ARSÈNE WENGER • CLIVE WOODWARD • USAIN BOLT

# Winners - Alistair Campbell

SCORE: 79%

OUTLINE: How sports stars, entrepreneurs and individuals win.

REVIEW: This book is similar to 'Outliers' by Malcom Gladwell. Campbell takes several case studies from sports and politics in which people have employed fairly straight forward and simple techniques to succeed at the highest levels. There are examples of campaign managers, for Obama v's Clinton, and their use of data and analytics. A look into Team Sky and their usage of 'marginal gains' to dominate the sport. It is an interesting read but if you have already read the books I have previously reviewed then it may be a refresher on some principles with different case studies rather than some ground breaking concepts and theories.

# 8. MOTIVATION.

*The fire to start, keep going and NEVER quit!*

Uhh. Sometimes you just want to give up, right? 'I cant be arsed' or 'It's not working like I thought it would'. Come on, everyone has been here at some stage of their life surely? If you think back to something like riding a bike it might be one of your earlier memories or you might not recall it. Either way the vast majority of people can ride a bike and that is because at the time we probably had either someone helping and coaching us along or we had nothing but sheer passion and determination to succeed.

I suppose the older you get the more you start to accept the status quo and you start to forgive yourself for not achieving certain things. It's sad really because those 'things', be it a bucket list goal, a promotion, a date with a new person, a personal best on the track or in the gym, are the type of reinforcing behaviours that subsequently lead us to achieve even more. The reward of the success develops our confidence in the attainment of our goals and that positive self rewarding prophecy continues to develop leading to even more confidence, more attainment and more motivation.

So confidence can help contribute towards motivation but it's certainly not the only thing that enhances motivation. Consider goal setting for instance. If you have effectively set goals, covered in another chapter of this book, and those goals have been broken down into attainable chunks then the motivation required to achieve one of your sub goals will be relatively easy compared to the instance where you may have just been handed the large overall task. You don't just run a marathon, you run 26 sequential miles and each of those miles are run one step at a time. So goal setting helps with motivation, confidence helps and aligning your task with your value or needs helps. Let's illustrate this with the marathon analogy. ANYONE, able bodied or not, can run or cover a marathon. ANYONE! It's just a matter of finding the motivation or aligning it with your needs. At this point I can hear you saying "well I can't run a marathon". So let me take a moment to motivate you by matching the marathon to one of your needs, like survival.

We all have an innate need to survive so do you think you could run a marathon if I held a gun to your head and chased you the whole way round? I think you probably could and I bet you'd run four marathons back to back if I held a gun to the head of someone you really loved and cared about wouldn't you? Congratulations you're now an ultramarathon athlete! Look I know it's a stark example but the point that I am making is that if you can find a way to link your task, or objective, to your values, or your needs, then motivation will naturally follow. "I don't want to go to work" - but you will go because you need the money to survive and sustain your lifestyle. So the money in this case becomes your motivation but there are people volunteering in much harder roles than what you're working in because the task they are doing aligns with their values. And the attainment of their goals, the fulfilment of their values and the confidence they get as a result all develop feed their motivation to do it.

There are a raft of scientific studies that will illustrate the endorphins released into your body after the successful attainment of a long term goal but sometimes, even if you have found something you really want to do, you've broken into manageable chunks and your confident about doing it, life still finds a way of getting in the way! OK, so if you feel like this is happening to you or can see it in someone you know then some of the following titles are the ones that are going to help you straight back out of that rut.

Firstly, if you are in denial about being in a rut then 'The Dip' is a great title to identify exactly what it is happening. 'The Tipping Point' is great to identify that there is usually one single point, sadly not visible, where the decision to carry on leads to reward and the decision to stop leads to failure. The books in this chapter will be the FUEL TO YOUR FIRE!

Now if you are a 'stiff upper lip' English type then, 'Hello!' I have been there and I am with you. It's easy to be sceptical about all this 'happy crappy mumbo jumbo'. BUT stay with me for a moment. If you take a book by Grant Cardone, also in this chapter, and you pick up just a modicum of his energy then you will be UNSTOPPABLE.

You know the feeling you get when you see someone achieving something you admire? A moment of inspiration where you feel you could replicate their achievement and their effort. Well use some of the titles in this chapter to give you that stimulus. Use them to help you develop your level of motivation and your desire to push through the hard times and hit the target that you're aiming for. These books and what they contain will help you go from average to extraordinary if you match it with your new found motivation.

The problem with average is that it is fucking boring. Yeah it's safe but really do you want to end up on you death bed saying 'I played it safe and now, well, I'm going to die anyway'? Be the person that does something excellent, leaves a legacy, works hard and shows real GRIT in their aim to succeed. Turn up, put the work in, show all those people with their self entitlement philosophy that they can stick it right up their self entitled fucking arse!

The author Frank Dick wrote about successful, motivated people in the book 'Winning' and his main point is that winners are mountain people. They climb a mountain and when they get to the top they want to climb another mountain. The opposite are valley people. They stay at the bottom scared of the elements and they play it safe in their comfort bubble. If you need some help staying motivated it's all here for you ready to go. Be a mountain person!

| | |
|---|---|
| Drive | Daniel Pink |
| 10X Rule | Grant Cardone |
| Tipping Point | Malcom Gladwell |
| The Dip | Seth Godin |
| How To Stay Motivated | Zig Ziglar |
| How to be Fucking Awesome | Dave Meredith |
| Be Obsessed or Be Average | Grant Cardone |
| The Alchemist | Paulo Coelho |

"Provocative and fascinating." —MALCOLM GLADWELL

# Daniel H. Pink

author of *A Whole New Mind*

DRiVE

The Surprising Truth
About What Motivates Us

# Drive - Daniel H Pink

SCORE: 82%

OUTLINE: Tips and tricks on how to help motivate people.

REVIEW: In this book the author looks at what it is that motivates individuals. How different levels and influences of motivation can be observed in people and how identifying these can help you harness that motivation. If you need to motivate people, or yourself, as a part of a team, or alone, this book is certainly worth a read. It's like a genuine management style book that's as applicable to the individual as it is to the team leader.

THE ONLY DIFFERENCE BETWEEN SUCCESS AND FAILURE

# THE 10X RULE

GRANT CARDONE

*NEW YORK TIMES* BESTSELLING AUTHOR OF
*IF YOU'RE NOT FIRST, YOU'RE LAST*

# The 10 X Rule - Grant Cardone

SCORE: 90%

OUTLINE: Adrenaline for your Motivation.

REVIEW: It's the 10 X rule baby! What ever you're doing, it ain't enough! Listen to this book and Grant Cardone will give you the biggest kick up the arse you've had since your parents got hold of your flailing report card when you were a kid! If you think you could be more productive, more motivated or more anything then he's going to tell you you could! If you ever saw the film 'Limitless' and afterwards felt that nothing was impossible then you're going to love the effect this book has as well! If you have a huge goal, project, task, effort or miracle you need to achieve read this book first. You'll probably get it done 10X faster!

# The
# TIPPING POINT

*How Little Things Can*
*Make a Big Difference*

## MALCOLM
## GLADWELL

*"A fascinating book that makes you see the world*
*in a different way."* —FORTUNE

# The Tipping Point - Malcom Gladwell

SCORE: 93%

OUTLINE: Crossing that invisible line between quitting and winning. When, where, why and how does it happen?

REVIEW: What an Author! This author can captivate you in his documentary style writing as he explains phenomenon that are seemingly unnatural. In this title he looks at the invisible line that one has to cross, but can not see, that will see your efforts rewarded and the benefits start to roll in. Business owners who are on the verge of giving up may also be on the verge of breaking through but sometimes they just can't see this invisible tipping point moment. If you could see or quantify the 'tipping point' then motivation to continue would never be an issue. There are case studies where some have given up and where some have pushed through and won. A great read.

# the dip

A LITTLE BOOK THAT
TEACHES YOU WHEN TO QUIT
(AND WHEN TO STICK)

Bestselling author of *Purple Cow* and *Small Is the New Big*

## SETH GODIN

# The Dip - Seth Godin

SCORE: 75%

OUTLINE: Identifying that rut when the novelty has worn off.

REVIEW: 'The Dip' focuses on the concept that after initially taking up a past time, hobby, career, profession etc there is a "dip" phase where the level of interest is reduced as the progress rate slows. This 'dip' region is critical to identify as once you know that you are in some kind of 'rut', you can identify it and work through it. Think of the example of a student in any subject. They'll go on a course, learn some new facts, legislations, techniques etc and then off they go to build on their project. But enroute they become demotivated by set backs and lack of progression or tangible results. THIS IS THE DIP. The goals and results are out there, play the long game and don't give up, use people around you to help. This book will help you identify what's happening and other books such as 'The Tipping Point' and 'The Law of Success' will help sustain you. It may also help to identify big picture goals and values with help from 'The Values Factor' by John DeMartini.

# How To Stay Motivated - Zig Ziglar

SCORE: 81%

OUTLINE: A motivational refresher to keep you on track and on task.

REVIEW: Zig Ziglar keeps you on top of your goals in an excitable manner. In this book there is a focus on maintaining your drive but only for what is right for you. There is a section that focuses on the positive use of language that, no doubt, would be heavily endorsed by NLP experts, and how this is especially important for people at/in a developing age/environment. The book is divided into 3 sections with Zig Ziglar taking section 1 and 3. Section 2, by Larry Iverson, looks at pre-visualisation, a mental rehearsal method used commonly by professional athletes. What's good about this book is that it guides you through a pre-visualisation exercise rather than just discussing the topic, which is great if you've never done it before.

The authors continually recommend listening to the book 16 times in total so that it totally sinks in. Your choice I suppose!

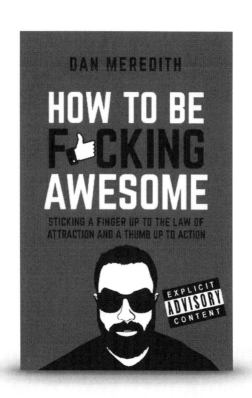

# How To Be Fucking Awesome - Dan Meredith

SCORE: 89%

OUTLINE: A big kick up the ass for those who just don't 'do'.

REVIEW: In this book the author takes a bit of a stick to some of the more spiritual methods of achieving things in life. He acknowledges that it's about balance but sometimes you do just have to get on with shit and get stuff done. This book is a bit like having Gary Vaynerchuck, a motivational speaker and life coach to the millennial generation, giving you a 4 hour stern talking to. It's rough but it's valid and I think there are a lot of procrastinators that need to hear this in their life. They would do well to heed the advice but I expect most will continue the way they are.

BE OBSESSED

OR BE AVERAGE

GRANT CARDONE

Bestselling author of *THE 10X RULE*

# Be Obsessed Or Be Average - Grant Cardone

SCORE: 90%

OUTLINE: An adrenaline shot to the heart of your motivation Grant Cardone style!

REVIEW: If you've read Grant Cardone 10x rule and it gave you a KICK up the arse then this book will be the sequel that fuels the beast even more! This guy has so much energy it's insane! But if you can harness and absorb 1% of it you'll be 10x more productive after reading it than before. Cardone endorses obsession(s) and encourages the development and maintenance of them to keep your 10x lifestyle going. A lot of the book is based on sales and generation of sales, this may seem a little irrelevant at points if you don't have a business but there are obvious metaphors to be read from all examples. There are a lot of one liners in the book that you could definitely 'bank' in your mind and keep hold of them for times when you feel like giving up. One thing Cardone points out is that, in fact, when you feel like giving up your brain is telling you that 'you could', but 'you have an option'. NEVER, EVER QUIT and you can only win.

# The Alchemist - Paulo Coelho

SCORE: 77%

OUTLINE: A classic encounter with a motivational message.

REVIEW: Have a dream/ambition/goal and do EVERYTHING to pursue it. You're better off dead along the way than dying someday just existing. Learn from what life throws at you, be humble in your victories, think of the big picture and NEVER, EVER, EVER give up! The religious metaphors can be a little off putting at times if you're not keen on religion but if you see through the metaphors then the message is useful.

# 9. PURPOSE.

*Helping you figure out yours if you don't already know.*

When I was a child I never had a clear idea of what I wanted to be when I grew up. I never had any major inspiration on fantastic careers and I can say that in school my 'careers development officer' only ever hindered my progress. On the two times that my school organised 'work experience', a project where school kids go out and work for a week in order to got an idea of what different jobs are like, I asked both times to go to a military base that involved some element of flying and both times I was told it wasn't possible and so one week found myself working in a sports retail shop and another week painting wooden 'for sale' posts a yellow colour for a sign company. I suppose at least this showed me that I didn't want to go into either of these professions.

I can't say that I had a strong sense of purpose. I do remember the admiration I felt when I met a friend, who was a high level sailing athlete, and that gave me the drive to follow start rowing. But what kept me rowing? For seven years I rowed almost every day rising early, often in my later teen life, after a night out socialising and drinking, in the early hours to cycle 9 miles to get to a rowing club. Then I'd start the gruelling training regime and cycle home. This level of intensity became even stronger at university where I was completing 35 hours a week of training alongside studying.

You can break a lot of things down by asking who, what, when, where, why, how? 'What' I wanted to do was clear, be an Olympic rower. Where, when and how were all pretty clear as well through a structured training regime but 'why' and 'who' highlight the purpose behind it all. Deep down I wanted to be admired the same way that I had admired my sailing friend, quite simple really and that purpose drove me continuously. I never became an olympian and one day my coach proved that, owing really to my physiology, I never would be. My coach seat raced me against rowers in the first eight, I was in the second eight (second best boat on the team of around eight or nine boats), and I got my arse handed to me on a plate, by a few guys who did end up becoming olympians. It was hard at the time but it moved me on and my next big challenge which was following an aviation career in the Royal Air Force. Don't underestimate how much harder that is than becoming an Olympian! It's a lot harder! However, again, when a lot of other people would have, and in fact did, throw in the towel and quit I persisted in aviation, despite having no natural ability at it, because I had purpose. This time the purpose had come from admiring the characters from the movie Top Gun and admiring a plane doing aerobatics, that I watched from a beach one day in Devon.

Whilst these 'identities' were my purpose at the time, I never actually realised it. I didn't deconstruct my behaviours and analyse them to figure it out. It was only decades later after leaving the Royal Air Force and starting to read books that I figured it out and by this time I had got older and subsequently realised my purpose had moved on. I expect as most people get older they change their priorities, quite naturally, as the progress through different milestones and stages of their lives. The things that drove me then are not the same things that drive me now but the point is that I had a sense of purpose, even if i didn't know it, and it helped me push through not only the hardest challenges I ever faced but seemingly harder challenges than other people were facing.

How many times have you heard, or felt yourself, that you just don't know what your purpose is? I hear it a lot and often I think people are just hoping one day that the answer just presents itself to them. If you are struggling to identify your purpose or know someone that is then the following titles will help no end.

As a starting point I would kick off with 'Start With Why'. It highlights the reasons of how powerful knowing this is and it will certainly give you the motivation to figure out your 'Why'. But if you only read one book from this whole chapter then I suggest 'The Values Factor' but it comes with a warning label. It's one of the best and also one of the hardest books I have ever read. It will take time, effort and work to get through it but the results are phenomenal. I can't stress enough here though that the results of this title only come when you complete the book and all the exercises. I have very motivated friends who have started and never completed this book and have thus wasted their time so only tackle it if you really have the absolute unrelenting urge to find out your purpose in life. It's tough but it's worth it.

Discovering your purpose will help you stay focused, it will make you passionate about achieving your goals and it will give you a greater sense of clarity, especially in times of adversity. There are other benefits as well though. If you know your purpose and you act in accordance with it then you'll end up living a more gratified life. Naturally if you do something you hate every day it's not hard to see how you'll become resentful about your situation. No one wants to hang around with that miserable prick!

We all know of someone that lives in a way that illustrates their purpose and value and those people seem to have an integral flow of grace in what they do making them easy to trust and fun to be around.

In one way or another rather following books should help you identify, develop or inspire your sense of purpose and the power in knowing it will give you a great sense of strength in pushing forward with other elements of your life.

| | |
|---|---|
| Start With Why | Simon Sinek |
| The Values Factor | John DeMartini |
| Tribes | Seth Godin |
| Mans Search For Meaning | Victor Frankl |
| The Gratitude Effect | John DeMartini |

# START

## HOW GREAT LEADERS INSPIRE
## EVERYONE TO TAKE ACTION

# WITH

## SIMON SINEK

*New York Times* bestselling author of *Leaders Eat Last* and *Together Is Better*

# WHY

# Start With Why - Simon Sinek

SCORE: 90%

OUTLINE: If you're going to start a journey it's probably best you know where and why you're going there. If not, you'll never arrive.

REVIEW: The book looks at why some people and organisations are more innovative, more influential, and more profitable than others? Why do some command greater loyalty from customers and employees alike? Even among the successful, why are so few able to repeat their successes over and over? Essentially, if you have a strong sense of why and you communicate that message then you can attain cult like loyalty and go from good to great. Don't confuse 'why' with 'where' either. Knowing where you want to go will get you somewhere efficiently, knowing why will keep you going when everyone else has quit.

THE
VALUES
FACTOR

The SECRET to CREATING an
INSPIRED and FULFILLING LIFE

DR. JOHN DEMARTINI

# The Values Factor - Dr John DeMartini

SCORE: 100%

OUTLINE: GAME CHANGER ! If you don't know what you want, READ THIS !

REVIEW: This book is one of a few game changers! Definitely in my top ten all time books and it has so much value if you read it and complete the associated exercises. I'm not going tell you this book is an easy listen. It isn't. In fact you will have to really concentrate and work hard, there are a lot personal searching questions for you to answer, repeatedly, but I can guarantee you it will be worth it. If you complete the whole book, as I have recommended to so many of my close friends, and if you complete it with those who are close to you, you will be able to identify, through self-objective analysis, what your current values are. Even if you think you don't know them this book will help you identify them. Then, if you feel you want to change your values, it will give you some helpful guidance in how to do so. One of the BIGGEST lessons John DeMartini taught me in this book was how knowing your values, and that of say, your significant other, can help you lead a relationship with more understanding. I whole heartedly suggest anyone read this book. It's LONG and it needs work but I promise you it's time very well spent.

# Tribes - Seth Godin

SCORE: 83%

OUTLINE: How people have created a following tribe and why.

REVIEW: Middle managers fear change and use their role to cut costs and improve statistics. Leaders, true leaders will take a tribe of people and get them to go above and beyond because they believe in the leaders idea or concept, the leaders 'why'. Monetisation is usually just a bi-product of their success and not the initial aim. Tribes will normally go out of their way to spread your message and it's because they believe in the cause. If you know your 'why' and you can communicate that purpose, or mission, to your team/following, you'll garner unstoppable momentum.

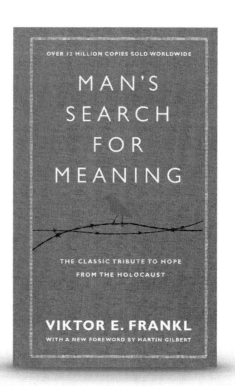

OVER 12 MILLION COPIES SOLD WORLDWIDE

# MAN'S SEARCH FOR MEANING

THE CLASSIC TRIBUTE TO HOPE
FROM THE HOLOCAUST

## VIKTOR E. FRANKL

WITH A NEW FOREWORD BY MARTIN GILBERT

# Mans Search For Meaning. - Viktor Frankl

SCORE: 88%

OUTLINE: A holocaust survivor's account of prisoner psychology.

REVIEW: This is a really interesting read. A man sentenced to his death in a concentration camp, who survived by fate, many separate times, accounts how the prisoners reacted to the most inhumane treatment imaginable. There are accounts of how quickly one becomes desensitised and how personal survival lead to cannibalism in some cases. The author also illustrates that knowing your purpose can maintain your resilience. If you think you need some perspective on life then this book will open your eyes for sure!

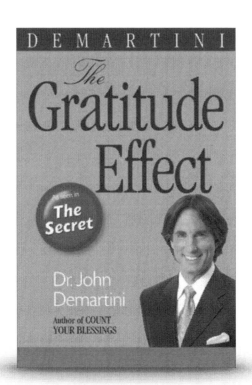

As seen in
**The Secret**

DEMARTINI

*The*
Gratitude
Effect

Dr. John
Demartini

Author of COUNT
YOUR BLESSINGS

# The Gratitude Effect - John Demartini

SCORE: 85%

OUTLINE: The effects of appreciation.

REVIEW: Some overlap from Values Factor in case studies and some links to The Secret. Sometimes this seems to be an advert through out for attending a Demartini workshop called 'The Break Through'. However, cynicism aside, if you apply the gratitude effect, that a LOT of self help books endorse, then I can't see there really being any negative side to it. People will probably just like you more and you'll be more chilled out. Say thanks, actually be thankful and appreciate all that you already have. Again, with Demartini, he looks at your purpose and how being grateful in daily life can assist you with development in that area.

# 10. PERSPECTIVE.

*Get some! No one has too much of it.*

It's very easy to stay inside our own bubble all the time. We can walk around all day worrying about what it is that is affecting us and this is natural, but it is not altogether that healthy. There are different levels of stress and some of these are covered really well in the Healthy Living chapter of this book. Essentially though our stress is driven by what we perceive it is that is affecting us. Your mind is geared to be alert for stress and there are evolutionary reasons behind this so you're not going to shake them off anytime soon but what we can do is try and put our stress into perspective a little more and in doing so reduce the amount of stress that we are susceptible to.

Having a broader perspective is normally something that we would associate with age and the variety of experience that age brings. But you don't always have to experience things to get some perspective on things. In fact waiting for perspective to occur is about the slowest way possible. Watching films, documentaries, reading books and talking to people are all ways in which a different perspective can be communicated to you. For now I can help with the books.

Some of the authors in this chapter will certainly be able to enhance the perspective that you already have and open up your mind into considering a whole different world of possibility, scale and more.

To start with, Malcom Gladwell can illustrate in 'Outliers' why considering something like the date of birth of your future off sprig, and subsequently perhaps when you decide to try and conceive, might be worth considering. I thought when you were born would have no impact on how you did in life but it turns out your birthday might actually be more profound than you thought.

'Homo Deus' is the sequel to another fascinating book that will have you considering how to map out your future now that you have a little more perspective on the changes that are likely to head in the direction of us mere mortals. And have you ever considered immortality, really thought it might be possible?

A diversified perspective can ultimately help in a lot of areas of your life especially decision making, reasoning, empathy and problem solving where, if you have a bigger picture of what's going on, you'll be in a position to make more informed answers. For instance if you're looking to employ someone or spend more time in a relationship with someone and that person is, say for instance, an endurance athlete you may be put off, as a potential employer or partner, because of the likely time away that person may need to be afforded. If you have read some of the books contained in this chapter though you may learn about some of the mindsets that their past time develops in them. You may then consider the decision to hire or date them quite differently knowing that they are a committed, determined individual who will never quit on a task regardless of the effort involved.

Increased perspective may also help you figure out your own goals. It may help you with setting, maintaining and achieving them as you learn from other people what is really possible, realistic and achievable.

And what is it that we are all actually trying to do and achieve and aim for? If you find yourself pondering these questions and getting concerned over them then the final books may give some perspective one how much of an impact you are likely to make on this planet that we occupy. The vastness of the World and everything beyond it can be incomprehensible but there are some books that do a great job in highlighting what actually exists and how small sometimes your own little personal bubble is.

The aim of gaining perspective is not to reduce the importance of what you do or to minimise the impact that you make. What you do can make a profound difference to other people, good and bad. You can deliberately cause suffering or satisfaction on others daily. The aim is to get you to destress a little and realise that some things are way out of your control and so they are barely worth thinking about let alone stressing about to the point of causing negative physiological symptoms.

If you have a narrow focus in life you may miss the bigger picture, and we all know how frustrating is to deal with someone if they are narrow minded. A wider outlook will help you capture and integrate more factors within the solutions that you come up with. Remembering *why* you are doing an activity, as with goal setting and motivation, means maintaining the subsequent *how* will be far easier.

Finally be open to considering other peoples' issues as well as your own. This development of perspective will naturally encourage a development of genuine empathy. You never know how bad someone else might actually have it and this may help you appreciate how good you actually have it as well.

Outliers                          Malcom Gladwell

The Monk Who Sold His Ferrari     Robin Storme

What Doesn't Kill Us              Scott Carney

Homo Deus                         Yuval Noah Horari

David and Goliath                 Malcom Gladwell

The Inevitable                    Kevin Kelly

The Theory Of Everything          Stephen Hawkins

God is Not Great                  C. Hitchens

'Inspiring,
revelatory'
THE TIMES

The No. 1 International Bestseller

# OUTLIERS

*The* STORY *of* SUCCESS

# MALCOLM GLADWELL

Author of *The Tipping Point* and *Blink*

# Outliers - Malcom Gladwell

SCORE: 93%

OUTLINE: Naturally Talented? Afraid not! An insight as to how and why the successful really are successful.

REVIEW: So you think that some people are born with talent? WRONG !!!! This book looks at how many circumstantial events are almost ALWAYS the result of the apparently supernatural. Gladwell highlights how if you want to have a confident child, who is successful at sports and has the best advantages in life then you can go a LONG way towards it by planning the time of year that you will give birth! About 80% of all Canadian professional ice hockey players are born in September and the remaining 20% in October and November. Not born in those months; sorry you probably won't make it. If that sounds ridiculous to you then read this book. There are many other case studies to highlight that people are not 'born with it'.

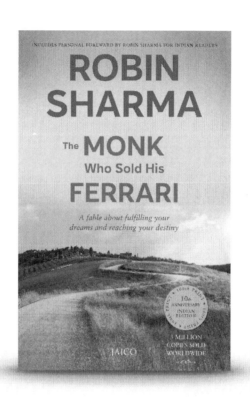

# The Monk Who Sold His Ferrari - Robin Sharma

SCORE: 78%

OUTLINE: A lawyer turned spiritual evangelist although not Christian.

REVIEW: This book has some really good stories/fables/anecdotes to illustrate why sometimes material and financial wealth should not be the sole aim in life but rather be included in part of a balanced and moderated life. A lawyer has a life changing health event that leads him to a pilgrimage involving monks. There he learns some life lessons and returns to impart them on to his friends and loved ones. It's almost certainly worth a read if only to make you take a step back and analyse what you're focusing on and if that could do with a little or large re-evaluation. The book may give you a bit more perspective through its fictional narrative and is less of a 'how to' and more of an insight provider.

HOW FREEZING WATER, EXTREME ALTITUDE, AND ENVIRONMENTAL CONDITIONING WILL RENEW OUR LOST EVOLUTIONARY STRENGTH

# WHAT DOESN'T KILL US

SCOTT CARNEY

FOREWORD BY WIM HOF

# What Doesn't Kill Us - Scott Carney

SCORE: 80%

OUTLINE: Life has become soft.

REVIEW: The author looks into some training and events that are extreme but that have theoretical concepts that underpin their validity. He meets the founder of the tough mudder movement and highlights how he failed to capitalise it. He also studies under Wim Hoff- THE ICE MAN, and follows him up Mount Kilimanjaro without any clothes on. He is a convert who wanted to examine the physiological benefits to living a bit more Neanderthal. Key take away is that we are all a little soft and that if you embrace the seasons, shirtless, you might actually help your body develop specific fats that can be good for you. A very interesting book to give you perspective on what the human body can actually cope with and not what our limited minds impose on it.

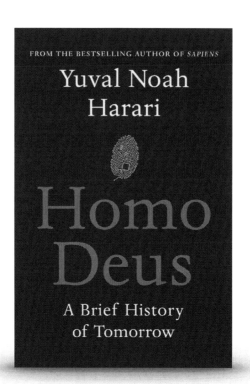

FROM THE BESTSELLING AUTHOR OF *SAPIENS*

Yuval Noah
Harari

Homo
Deus

A Brief History
of Tomorrow

# Homo Deus - Yuval Noah Harahi

SCORE: 91%

OUTLINE: An incredibly eye opening book in to a world beyond liberalism and into data-ism.

REVIEW: The author in this book picks up from the title Homo Sapiens, by the same author, and looks at the future of the human race as supposed to the history of it. There are a lot of thoroughly philosophical debates that will contend with strong religious and spiritual believers and they are not the only people who will find this uncomfortable reading. A lot like the book 'Inevitable' the book covers the future of the likely labour market when coupled with the development of AI. It evaluates the values humans hold and how they differ from the values that animals and computers hold. Is life an algorithm itself or will it be taken over by them? And specifically, if you want to know yourself, and I mean really know yourself, ask Google! Confused? Read the book and all will be clear!

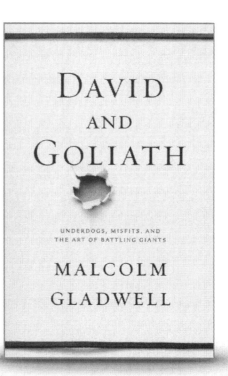

# David And Goliath - Malcom Gladwell

SCORE: 85%

OUTLINE: Another fantastically interesting book from Malcom Gladwell.

REVIEW: Gladwell, in this book, looks at some of the common myths that surround 'David and Goliath' style battles. He deconstructs commons myths and then analyses why sometimes an impossible task is actually achievable and the common cause and effects of the 'David' winners. He also looks at the subsequent affects of good intentions and how then can, sometimes, result in a counterproductive unintended consequence. 'Can't' is the real 'C' word and this book will give you some perspective on how you might be able to achieve it.

NEW YORK TIMES BESTSELLER

# THE INEVITABLE

UNDERSTANDING
THE 12 TECHNOLOGICAL
FORCES THAT
WILL SHAPE OUR
FUTURE

## KEVIN KELLY

AUTHOR OF *WHAT TECHNOLOGY WANTS*

# The Inevitable - Kevin Kelly

SCORE: 80%

OUTLINE: The future. Probably.

REVIEW: A very interesting insight into the author's view of what the future will hold for us all. There are some great concepts of how AI and automation will evolve and how tech will become far more embedded than it already is in our lifestyles. There is some good information on crypto currencies and why now may be the best time to get involved in some of the these things. Quite interesting as well is the view that there is a strong possibility that we will end up as a social global state where we will eventually have to be paid to exist as the job market will entirely change.

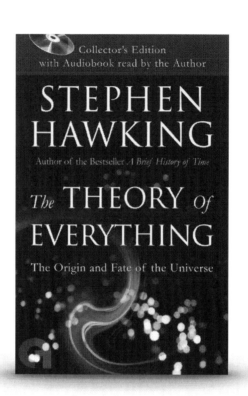

# The Theory Of Everything  - Stephen Hawkins

SCORE: 70%

OUTLINE: Get ready to have your mind blown.

REVIEW: WAY OVER MY HEAD ! Perhaps it's just that I am a simple person that deals better with tangible things or numbers or that I am not used to listening to this subject matter. Either way I can't listen to this audio on double speed, as I normally would, as it stretches my thought process on the abstract topic of the universe, quantum physics and black holes.  What the book will do though is make you appreciate just how small and irrelevant our impact on the universe is. Yes, you can affect you fellow humans and you can inflict good or bad situations on others BUT if you think you'll make a dent on the world then think again. Even a global movement will have very small effects.

THE #1 *NEW YORK TIMES* BESTSELLER

"Written with tremendous brio and great wit . . .
an all-out attack on all aspects of religion."
Michael Kinsley, *New York Times Book Review*

god

is not

# Great

How Religion Poisons Everything

Christopher
Hitchens

With a New Afterword

# God Is Not Great - Christopher Hitchens

SCORE: 85%

OUTLINE: A good read if you're a religious believer.

REVIEW: The author presents some very balanced, logical and sound arguments as to why religion is largely a made up human construct. It is contradictory, inconsistent and can be proved, scientifically, to be grossly flawed. The source of religious disputes have lead to the vast majority of terror attacks and those that claim they are political disputes can be traced back to religion. Some westerners are shocked by extreme Islamists who claim not to be homosexual paedophiles and yet sodomise young boys on Thursdays, for fun, and those people are equally shocked by western catholic priests who, on mass, have done very similar things to the youth they are supposed to influence and protect. When they are found out they are discreetly moved to different parishes where they are likely to get away with it, again. By far the most ridiculous claims though seem to be that master-bating causes blindness and that hurricane Catrina in the USA was the result of legalisation of gay marriage. It presents some interesting arguments that it would be interesting to hear a religious preacher rebut.

# 11. GOALS.

*Set, track, attain.*

Having a goal is great. Achieving a goal can be quite another thing altogether and it is achieving them that this chapter sets out to help with. There are a hundred different cliches like 'A goal that is not achieved is just a dream' and whilst they sound a bit trite, there is some truth behind it. It's a fairly niche subject within the self development genre and that is, in my opinion, because it really isn't complicated enough to justify a whole book. There are several other titles that will deal with goal setting and achievement as a chapter within a book but if you found you want a little more material on the subject then hopefully you can find it here.

'Focal Point' is a really good read as is 'Unstoppable' and the two authors will take you through techniques that will help you identify your goals, write them down and then start to break the bigger goals down into smaller sub categories. All of this is designed to make it easier to obtain for your mind and thus remove the roadblocks on the way to your achievement.

If I could sit down with my 18 year old self I would suggest he writes down all of his goals and aspirations somewhere. The simple act alone of writing them down will start to help encourage the repetition of these goals in the mind. I'll digress here for a moment but its a valid point so bear with me. 'The Secret' is a book that essentially endorses the fact that if you *think* of something enough and you positively envisage it with your mind then it will happen. Honestly, I think they have done a great job on the marketing and sales of the book, but in large the book is a ton of shit. Alas you won't find me ever recommending it. Now before I alienate all of the avid followers/cult members that follow it, I will say that the act of thinking about something does have some merit in achieving a goal. If you always think about becoming a famous singer then I'm sure you'll be the person that notices the singing lesson advert and you'll sign up to start your journey. So having the goal in your mind helped inspire you to *start* the journey. But thinking of being the next Ed Sheeran wasn't the thing that got you up every day to work on your craft. *Thinking* IS NOT determination, grit, perseverance, skill, practice, talent, commitment, and all the other traits required to be an expert in your field. So the only real secret about 'The Secret' is that thinking of something will start you on, maybe, 1% of your journey. For the rest of the journey you're going to have to turn up and put some skin into the game!

Anyway back to writing goals down. Do it! I had a ton of goals and dreams in my head when I was growing up. I suppose it's all part of what we do when we enter adult life and form our identity. But don't leave them up in your head. Get them down on paper and start to come up with a bit of a plan. How many times have you heard 'I always wanted to do that but...' Who wants to be the person who always has an excuse for why they have done something? If you write all your goals down, like I randomly did one day for a bit of fun, you'll find in front of you that you have something akin to a Bucket List. Commonly most people know of a Bucket List as a bunch of things, experiences or milestones we want to achieve before we die. So now we know you want to do it before you die we have some kind of time line. If you can't quite see what's happening here then I will let you in on one of the most popular goal setting acronyms. S.M.A.R.T (E.R) Goals.

S.M.A.R.T (E.R) Goals should be: Specific, Measurable, Attainable, Relevant and Timely. Some people also add that you should Evaluate and Reward your goals. Sometimes, depending on where you look, this acronym will use slightly different words but the common aim is to progress you towards achievement. So then this is to say that a goal should be something specific that you want to achieve and not ambiguous. I want to run a marathon rather than I want to take up running. It should be measurable, and a marathon is a specific measurement and it's attainable. Given the right motivation ANYONE can cover a marathon distance. Many people with physical and mental impairments run marathons so please don't let me hear the words 'I cant'. If running is relevant to you great, if it isn't then obviously pick something else. Finally it needs to be timely. This is to say we need some kind of timeline and timeframe. So lets say, in this example: I want to run a marathon by the end of this year in under 4 hours, I will evaluate my progress throughout my training and WHEN I complete my goal I will reward myself with a weekend in a spa (you'll need it after a marathon!)

The S.M.A.R.T.E.R theme will be laced throughout many of the book reviews here as well as suggesting that asking someone to hold you accountable will help with goal achievement and this can be done sometimes by declaring that you will do it on some social media platform. Then you have to do it because you told everyone you would! Right?

Once you're accountable you'll start. Track the sub-goals of the main goal as you achieve them, tick them off, this will in turn make you feel even better about your progress and help motivate you towards the next element. Before you know you know it BANG you've done it. You're Ed Sheehan or Mo Farah! You've climbed a mountain, run a marathon, written a book, lost your virginity, become a Hollywood actor and been President of the USA!

The biggest driver in all of the success though will be YOU. Even more specifically is the ACTION you take. As with many things in this book you're the only one who can kick things off, you're the only one who it really matters too and you're the only one who will really regret not doing it.

Finally DON'T EVER LET ANYONE TELL YOU THAT YOU CAN'T achieve one of your goals! Use that as fuel to keep you working towards your aim. Their doubt is usually because they don't think they could do it and are worried they'll feel insecure when you DO achieve it. Prove them wrong. SMASH IT! There really isn't any *secret* to it.

Focal Point                          Brian Tracey
Unstoppable                       Pete Wilkinson
Habit Stacking                    The Blokehead

BRIAN

A PROVEN SYSTEM

TRACY

TO SIMPLIFY YOUR LIFE, DOUBLE YOUR PRODUCTIVITY,

FOCAL

AND ACHIEVE ALL YOUR GOALS

POINT

# Focal Point - Brian Tracey

SCORE: 89%

OUTLINE: Rich content on how to improve your focus in order to achieve your real ambitions.

REVIEW: It's time to focus on the things that REALLY matter. In this book the author covers a vast array of pragmatic and practical advice on how you can refine your goal selection to best enable you to succeed in the areas you would like to be excellent in. One of the repeated questions posed is: Knowing what you now know what one thing would you change if you started again 20 years earlier? Figure out what that is and drop it now before you waste another 20 years. If you have already consumed a lot of self help books then there are some fantastic sections that revise these and if you're new to the topic prepare to have your mind blown with 100's of tips on how to improve your life. He discusses the law of reciprocity, characteristics of the successful, benefits of habitual behaviour, compound effect, paying yourself first and MANY more lifestyle improvement techniques that link strongly to working within property as an entrepreneur.

'Anyone who is fed up with being constantly busy but never getting the important stuff done should read this book. With Pete's straightforward action-plan, you'll soon regain your focus and start seeing the results you want!'
— Paul McGee, bestselling author of *Self-Confidence* and *S.U.M.O. (Shut Up, Move On)*

# UNSTOPPABLE
## USING THE POWER OF FOCUS TO TAKE ACTION AND ACHIEVE YOUR GOALS

### PETE WILKINSON

# Unstoppable - Pete Wilkinson

SCORE: 78%

OUTLINE: Using the power of FOCUS to take action and achieve your goals.

REVIEW: The author talks through, justifies and reasons, with the reference of many other self help and time management books, the need to set and maintain action towards goals. He takes you through his one page action plan that will help you identify your vision, core strategies, goals, relationships and so on. By writing these out and having them in front of you, you will constantly have a reminder, also best placed on portable devices so that it is with you in a more Mobile lifestyle. This is a good read and it comes with PDFs that you can fill out to help you bring the task to reality and then allow that document to hold you accountable.

# Habit Stacking - The Blokehead

SCORE: 77%

OUTLINE: 30 quick fire steps to help set and achieve goals.

REVIEW: This is a useful book for beginners to look into regarding goal setting and avoiding procrastination. The author has written a fairly short book which gives 30 steps to follow when considering how to set your goals and methods that you can employ, such as the title suggests, 'Habit Stacking', to help you execute these goals. Other tactics include the S.M.A.R.T technique, writing goals down, peak performance and mistakes to avoid when setting goals. The good thing about this book is that all the basics are in here and because it is a short book it won't be overwhelming when working through it. The bad side is that if you prefer more information and background then you'll need to look elsewhere. The key to make this book work will be the action that you take.

# 12. SUCCESS MINDSET.

*The clues that successful people have left for you.*

This is going to be one of my favourite chapters in this book and I honestly envy the people that get to read these books for the first time. Most of the titles in here were such huge game changers for me when I read them that they almost left me on a high, thinking of all the potential that I could unlock in myself that had probably lain dormant without me realising it.

You'll probably hear a lot of people say that successful people are lucky and that they were an overnight success. Well I call bullshit on that one. If you ask successful people how they got to where they are you'll probably find that the 'luck' they had was actually a combination of hard work, good timing and a team of people around them that are far more capable in their given discipline than the person who is leading the event, project, product, life etc. That person you might have spoken to probably has a growth mindset. Mindset is the key to success in many ways and if you haven't already heard of it you can normally classify people into one of two camps. You have either a growth mindset or a fixed mindset. People with a fixed mindset will have the belief that your luck in life is responsible for where you end up. They are likely to think that someones ability is something they were born with and that if you are dealt a bad hand in life then you just have to accept it and live that life.

A growth mindset is the polar opposite to this. A growth mindset is likely to contribute towards helping all the areas of your life that you'd naturally want to do well in like relationships, financial status, career progression and personal health. Someone with a growth mindset will see failure not as a reason to give up or to avoid a task in the first place but rather they will see it as an opportunity to learn why something didn't work, analyse why it happened, think how they can mitigate it happening again in the future and then, probably, try again and succeed.

Now I said that you'll typically find people fall into one of the two camps but it doesn't mean you have to stay there. I'll assume at this point that if you've bought this book for yourself you probably don't have a fixed mindset but you may find that occasionally you get a little fed up or tired of being someone who has a growth mindset and is always responsible for staying motivated, switched on and driven. You're not alone and there are books in here that will help boost your resolve and validate your persistent effort to drive forward. If, however, you were given this book it might mean that someone with a growth mindset gave it to you knowing that you have the potential within you to do so much more than you do. You probably have a report card that echos my entire, very average, academic performance with comments like 'a lot of unused potential' or 'wastes his energy on non academic pursuits'. The important thing is that if someone has reached out to you with this book then they believe in you as a person. They may see that you are in adverse situation and that you have the power to get out it and succeed rather than be a victim of your circumstance.

The books in this chapter are perfect for developing, bolstering and affirming your success and growth mindset. They are equally effective at inspiring you to wake up your potential, to not accept the status quo and to go and get what you want rather than what you think you deserve.

If you've got an entitlement mentality, or know someone who could do with having that beaten out of them, the book GRIT is P.H.E.N.O.M.E.N.A.L ! Angela does an incredible job of highlighting the fact that to be successful you need to be lucky... Ha! I'm joking! You need to work hard and have a little, or hopefully, a LOT of grit. The reason that this is fantastic news is that people who have typically had a tougher life, the ones who feel constantly beaten down by the system, are exactly the people whose 'disadvantaged' circumstances have developed grit within them. When they realise that they have this increasingly rare asset within them, they will realise that all of the shit that has happened to them might actually be the very thing that makes them unstoppable, because of their resilience, determination and resourcefulness.

Jack Canfield's 'Success Principles' is a bit like a success mindset bible. Honestly you could go a lot further in life by owning and repeatedly reading this book alone. I found the individual chapters so useful that I set up reoccurring reminders on my phone, each day, to endlessly repeat one of the principles that he discusses in each chapter. As a bench mark I haven't done that with any other book that I have read. One chapter title comes up each day and has done so on my phone for the last few years and I don't want to disable it.

If you think that life is just going to work out by hoping it will then perhaps you should quit reading this book now. Life is going to deal you some unfair shit sometimes 'the kind that will blindside you on some idle Tuesday afternoon' (Sunscreen - Baz Luhrmann. Listen to it.). The successful people in this life are the ones who get knocked down, embrace the lesson, get back up and keep on going. Use your obstacles as learning opportunities, forget about what other people think of you, and do what it is that you want to do. Grind, sweat, work and what ever you do NEVER, EVER, EVER, quit! You can do it.

| | |
|---|---|
| The Success Principles | Jack Cranfield |
| Grit | Angela Duckworth |
| The Law of Success | Napoleon Hill |
| 21 Secrets of Self Made Millionaires | Brian Tracey |
| Endure | Alex Hutchinson |
| The Obstacle is The Way | Ryan Holiday |
| Millionaire Success Habits | Dean Grizosi |
| Ego is The Enemy | Ryan Holiday |
| The Impulse Society | Paul Roberts |
| The Magic of Thinking Big | David Schwartz |

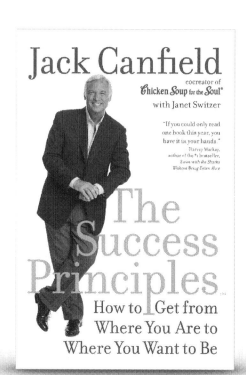

# Jack Canfield

cocreator of
**Chicken Soup for the Soul®**

with Janet Switzer

"If you could only read
one book this year, you
have it in your hands."
Harvey Mackay,
author of the #1 bestseller,
*Swim with the Sharks
Without Being Eaten Alive*

# The Success Principles™

## How to Get from Where You Are to Where You Want to Be

# The Success Principles - Jack Canfield

SCORE: 100%

OUTLINE: What it says on the tin. How to get from where you are to where you want to be.

REVIEW: AN EPIC BOOK!!! It's a bit like having 25 self help books rolled up into one. This book is definitely one of the longer books, at 21hrs, but certainly one of the better ones as well. If Self Improvement is new to you then the principles mentioned will be eye opening and give you a lot to think about. If you're more familiar with personal development it will be a great revision aide. Jack adds a personal insight to his journey and the gives examples of methods that have worked for him in the past and provides practical illustrations of how you can implement them into your life. The overall message is: Have goals, write them down, share them and most importantly TAKE ACTION. And if you only take one thing away from the book, in the words of the author, it will be the question "How would you rate this out of 10?". It will all make sense once you've read it.

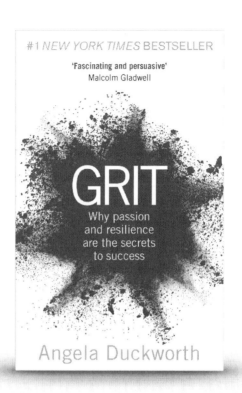

# Grit - Angela Duckworth

SCORE: 98%

OUTLINE: How the power of passion and perseverance can be harnessed, measured and developed.

REVIEW: Grit looks at what it takes to succeed in a plethora of disciplines and how you can determine that. Traditionally the use of academic scores, measures of physical strength or psychological evaluation may be tools used to predict someone chance of success. But it turns out, whilst those tools have their purpose, the measure of grit can tell who will persevere when times get tough, beyond the point that those who would seem capable normally give up. The author looks at how grit can be developed and where it fits into nature vs nurture. This book is a great read to help you summon a little more 'grit' when times get tough. If you're a lone entrepreneur and you're investing in property this book will serve as a good reminder to keep going.

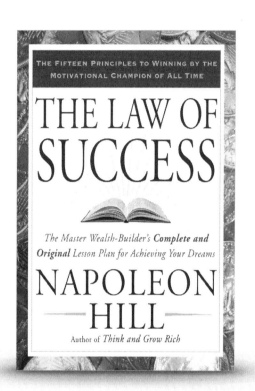

THE FIFTEEN PRINCIPLES TO WINNING BY THE
MOTIVATIONAL CHAMPION OF ALL TIME

# THE LAW OF
# SUCCESS

*The Master Wealth-Builder's* **Complete and
Original** *Lesson Plan for Achieving Your Dreams*

# NAPOLEON
# HILL

Author of *Think and Grow Rich*

# The Law of Success - Napoleon Hill

SCORE: 80%

OUTLINE: Put your achievable mind to it.

REVIEW: You can do it if you think you can. This book covers each of the 'laws' in great detail and its a good 24 hours long. I'd say a handful of books I have already read have based many of their principles on this books foundations therefore by reading and acting upon this book you may find your time efficiently spent despite its great length. The narration is reasonable quality but a WORD OF WARNING! This book was probably written nearly 100 years ago, the level of political correctness is apparent and whilst it is not intended to offend women or people from a variety of racial backgrounds it is undeniable that the labelling of individuals in this book would be deemed unacceptable by today's standards. Look past that though and take the book for its intended value and you will find some AMAZING lessons to take away.

THE
21 SUCCESS
SECRETS OF
$ELF-MADE
MILLIONAIRE$

HOW TO ACHIEVE FINANCIAL
INDEPENDENCE FASTER AND EASIER
THAN YOU EVER THOUGHT POSSIBLE.

BRIAN TRACY

# 21 Secrets Of Self Made Millionaires - Brian Tracey

SCORE: 83%

OUTLINE: Mindset to maintain enroute to success.

REVIEW: A great quick read through 21 Habits that are adhered to by successful people. Many of these quick revisions, or introductions if you are new to personal development, are whole topics in other books, so it's a great place to start if you want a brief insight. This book is the kind that you keep in your library as a great revision aide. The author looks at goal setting, development, perseverance, commitment, personal finance, being honest with yourself and how to get others on board with you as well as a host of other topics. You are not going to listen to this book and get rich, that's not the point of the title, but if you maintain these principles whilst working on what you're trying to achieve, monetarily or elsewhere, then I'm sure they will contribute towards success.

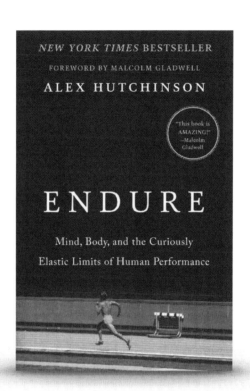

# Endure - Alex Hutchinson

SCORE: 91%

OUTLINE: How people persist.

REVIEW: Whether it's the determination to complete an Ultra Marathon or smash the marathon record of 2 hours, this book digs into it, and a lot more! It's SUCH an interesting read to see what it genuinely is that seems to drive, people, teams, companies and movements, to press on again and again and again against every plausible obstacle to achieve what is deemed impossible. Reading this, whilst enduring something yourself, will probably not only give you some perspective on your task, in relation to other examples of endurance, but also keep you going when you probably feel like quitting. It's a Malcom Gladwell style book that debunks myths and proves hard facts.

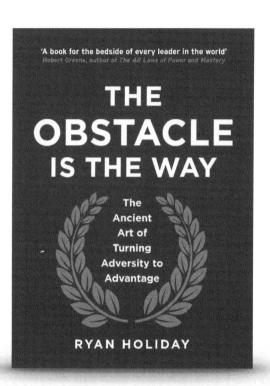

'A book for the bedside of every leader in the world'
Robert Greene, author of The 48 Laws of Power and Mastery

# THE
# OBSTACLE
## IS THE WAY

The
Ancient
Art of
Turning
Adversity to
Advantage

RYAN HOLIDAY

# The Obstacle Is The Way - Ryan Holiday

SCORE: 82%

OUTLINE: An obstacle can be as much of an opportunity as it can be a problem.

REVIEW: In this book the author highlights that when and where an obstacle comes up it can be far more beneficial to deal with it with a 'challenge' mind set rather than a defeatist one. Often an obstacle will be the end of the road for some people, be it on a journey, starting a business, changing their life etc. BUT if you consider those that didn't give up then what is evident is that the way to get somewhere you want to be is to overcome the obstacle and thus the obstacle becomes the way to go. Look for obstacles and relish in them. If someone says 'no' or 'can't or 'wont' then thank them for the opportunity they have given you to succeed at the point where everyone else has given up.

# Millionaire SUCCESS Habits

*The Gateway to Wealth & Prosperity*

FROM NY TIMES BEST SELLING AUTHOR
## DEAN GRAZIOSI

# Millionaire Success Habits - Dean Graziosi

SCORE: 91%

OUTLINE: Some life tips and tricks that have helped with the success of Millionaires.

REVIEW: I must say this book had a lot more content than I had expected. It looks like a bland self help title but the author actually delves into some great pragmatic advice that he has seen adopted by millionaire and billionaire business people that he knows and loves. There is helpful advice on topics such as personal development, finances, relationships, sales and marketing, philanthropy and more. I would thoroughly recommend this to anyone in any field as the examples are metaphorical as well as specific. Another reminder not to judge a book by its cover/title.

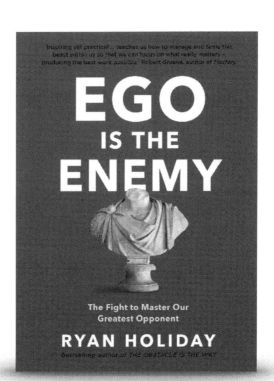

'Inspiring yet practical... teaches us how to manage and tame that
beast within us so that we can focus on what really matters –
producing the best work possible.' Robert Greene, author of *Mastery*

# EGO
## IS THE
# ENEMY

**The Fight to Master Our
Greatest Opponent**

## RYAN HOLIDAY

Bestselling author of *THE OBSTACLE IS THE WAY*

# Ego Is The Enemy - Ryan Holiday

SCORE: 87%

OUTLINE: Don't let your ego block your success and happiness.

REVIEW: This book contains lots of case studies highlighting how some of the great people of the past have succeeded when they have got out of the way of their ego, and equally great failures who have fallen a victim to theirs. One of the best lines is from a General who said "To Be, or, To Do". Essentially be ruled by your ego and become someone who wants 'TO BE' liked, admired and adored, notorious and to have notoriety or be someone whose aim is 'TO DO' something of notoriety and fame where it is not about them as the person but actually the act that is being committed. Your ego could be your worst enemy. By all means acknowledge it and harness its usefulness in motivation but perhaps drop the ostentatious character traits and materialistic life?

PAUL ROBERTS
BESTSELLING AUTHOR
OF *THE END OF OIL*

'I guarantee this will jog your thinking,
and perhaps put you on a new path'
**Bill McKibben, Author of *Enough***

'A brilliant feat of analytic journalism'
**Cullen Murphy, Editor at Large**
*Vanity Fair*

# THE
# IMPULSE
# SOCIETY
## WHAT'S WRONG WITH
## GETTING WHAT WE WANT?

BLOOMSBURY

# The Impulse Society - Paul Roberts

SCORE: 89%

OUTLINE: How the Instant Gratification Nation got to where it is and why.

REVIEW: This book highlights the course of actions that have slowly contributed to the Impulse Society of America. It looks at, in sometimes an evangelical fashion, how The USA has slipped into a nation of people who want everything, without working for it and they want it yesterday! It's not just America but the examples are State Side Centric. It is a great insight to how the industrial, banking, manufacturing, political and personal influences have shaped the modern person and more importantly why politicians and CEO's now have short term targets that often harm the long term outlook of their projects. I think if every CEO read this it would change the way they looked at things for about 5 seconds and then they would revert to type, EXACTLY for the reason that the book points out. A really interesting read and one that can certainly explain why you may be becoming less patient and how you may be able to cope/deal with it.

# The Magic Of Thinking Big. - David Schwartz

SCORE: 78%

OUTLINE: Think BIG !!!

REVIEW: Don't be constrained by small projects and a small mind set. It often only takes an adjustment to mindset to increase the type of projects taken on, pay rise sought, or ambition achieved, to achieve more. Think positively, use positive language, ban 'impossible' from your vocabulary. If you think you are weak you are, if you think you are inadequate you are, so if you think big in all aspects then you will be. Take the positive lessons and feedback from any failure. Nothing in this world is being done as well as it could be so think of improvements. In the words of the author "A wise man will be a master of his mind and a fool will be its slave".

# 13. PRODUCTIVITY.

*Getting more done with the most precious commodity, time.*

I know, I know, I know. You don't have time and you've probably got a lot on you plate right now. I don't think anyone can say they haven't said these words at some point. But if you really want to try and increase your productivity levels and free up a little more time for yourself then it might be worth taking some advice from people who have a whole load of suggestions, tips, hints and hacks on just how you can achieve that.

Effective productivity is almost a blend of good habits and time management, both of which are covered in previous chapters in this book. It allows you to either accomplish the same amount of things in less time or accomplish more things in the same amount of time, depending on what is more important for you. If you are productive it also gives you the feeling of being in control of your own time and by extension, of your own life. If this increased productivity is something that you can take into your work space, be that as an employee, an employer, an entrepreneur or solo-preneur, then you may actually find you are remunerated for your effort as well. It's not uncommon to see the most productive people receiving pay rises, bonuses or promotions and they may only be putting into place one or two basic concepts, contained within the following books, that no one has considered actioning before.

It's not just work life though that sees a real benefit. If your aim is to free up more time and you want to spend that time enhancing your family life, improving your ability in a sport or volunteering at a charity, then improving your productivity will enable you to gain a little more time freedom.

In this chapter there are some great titles that deal directly with productivity. The top three are 'Life Leverage' -Rob Moore, 'The Miracle Morning' -Hal Elrod and 'The 7 Habits of Highly Effective People' -Stephen Covey. Rob Moore will encourage you to really prioritise what it is that you need to do yourself and what tasks you can outsource to other people or indeed ones that you can drop. Stephen Covey discusses productivity enhancing habits that you can build into your daily routine. Then Hal Elrod will give you an incredibly effective way of actioning the whole thing by waking up early in the morning with a brilliant routine, that will include doing a ton of shit you've been putting off, all squared away before everyone else in the planet has even reached over to silence their alarm for the third time.

Productivity is all output and time related. In an economic context it is a measure of efficiency. One thing you'll find though is that you'll get better at being productive with more practice as well. As soon as you find one technique that works for you then you may use that new spare time to research another technique that you can implement. Eventually, and this is what is contained in these books, you'll have an artillery of different hacks and systems that will free up an abundance of time.

It's important to remember that being productive is not the same as simply being busy. Time management plays a part in it as does prioritisation, habit forming and the measuring of output. A plan for each day that contributes towards your overall plan for the week, month, year and so on, will be an effective way of working towards your end goals whilst also managing the day to day admin tasks. So, to avoid being busy you may need to focus a little more initially on the bigger picture tasks in life or work. Come up with a deliberate plan rather than just a simple job list. The later can be a great way to brain dump everything onto a piece of paper, so it has its value, but if you action a job list without prioritising you'll simply pick the easy ones first so that you have a feeling of self accomplishment when they are completed. Deep down though you know you need to prioritise the more important things first.

Being highly productive isn't easy, it's not something that just comes naturally for people. Sometimes you have to have a passion for what it is you're doing BUT there are a lot of productive people who simply apply a consistent routine to getting things done and who avoid crappy distractions in order to focus their efforts on that they know, or understand, to be really important. And for fuck sake can we just all try and grow up a little about it. Everyone has that job that they are putting off, it will be something niggling away in your mind that ends up occupying your brain space. You put it off longer and longer and longer and the bloody thing gets worse and worse. Develop some self discipline. Sit down and actually grind the fucking thing out until it's done. You and I both know that you'll feel loads better afterwards having done it. The endorphins will flow and you'll probably have a fantastic day afterwards. If you find you can't just sit down and do it then take a look at the following reviews. Pick the book that you think applies best to you then go off and get the book. Make sure once you've read it that you put the advice into action. I'm certain it will help you accomplish more in less time and allow you to control your time the way you want to.

| | |
|---|---|
| The 80/20 Principle | Richard Koch |
| The slight Edge | Jeff Olson |
| Life Leverage | Rob Moore |
| 7 Habits of Highly Effective People | Stephen Covey |
| The Miracle Morning | Hal Elrod |
| The Four Hour Work Week | Timothy Ferris |
| Deep Work | Cal Newport |

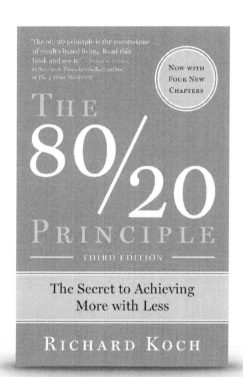

"The 80/20 principle is the cornerstone of results-based living. Read this book and use it." —Timothy Ferriss, #1 *New York Times* bestselling author of *The 4-Hour Workweek*

NOW WITH
FOUR NEW
CHAPTERS

# THE
# 80/20
# PRINCIPLE
—— THIRD EDITION ——

The Secret to Achieving
More with Less

RICHARD KOCH

# The 80/20 Principle - Richard Koch

SCORE: 80%

OUTLINE: A globally recognised principle explained!

REVIEW: Does what it says on the tin really. If you apply the principle you should become way more efficient in your work place/investments/productivity. At the end of the book it goes on to preview the humanistic and emotional aspects of the 80/20 Principle that I wasn't expecting. Basically have a few key, rich relationships and many acquaintances rather than having 100 best friends. Think about achieving more with less and whilst this is a nice thought I think that he slightly contradicts the compounding effect that he does, earlier on, endorse in the book. All in all this is a great explanation of the 80/20, Pareto's Law, concept and it provides real life scenarios that you can easily implement, if you choose to, in your own life.

# The Slight Edge- Jeff Olson

SCORE: 90%

OUTLINE: Get ready to recognise you can create a huge result with small incremental changes.

REVIEW: Basically make small positive changes to better your life. Are those changes easy to make? Yes. but are they easy to ignore? Absolutely. Persistence will beat resistance and everything is always in motion. You are either improving or degrading and although it may be, at first, an insidious change, the later effect of the seed you plant now will, after harvesting, grow with abundance. Avoid instant result and gratification mindset, work smart and most importantly invest in improving yourself and not your bowling score. 'The Slight Edge' is akin to the 'Marginal Gains' concept adopted by the highly successful Team Sky Cycling team and is widely endorsed.

The INSTANT TOP 10 BEST SELLER

'A great book that will change your life'
**BRIAN TRACY**
bestselling author of
*Eat That Frog*

# LIFE
# LEVERAGE

How to get more done in less time,
outsource everything and create
your ideal mobile lifestyle

## ROB MOORE

# Life Leverage - Rob Moore

SCORE: 97%

OUTLINE: How to get more done in less time.

REVIEW: If you have goal in life but everything seems to be getting in your way this will be a fantastic book for you. I have forwarded it onto the entrepreneurial people I know and those that run their own businesses. There are some great time hacks and life hacks in here that will enable you, if you action them, to free up more of your time and focus it on your passion. This book is, refreshingly, not filled with up-selling courses, something that is done in some of the other authors' books but rather it is filled with great content that will help all the self-improves out there.

Rob rightfully cites some of the great authors of the past that have illustrated fundamental principles and behaviours that get you ahead in life. He also came up with 'NETime' and there's a great bit about helping you realise your goals and what your time is actually worth. It's a great read and one I'd thoroughly recommend, regardless of whether or not you're an employee or employer.

# The 7 Habits Of Highly Effective People- Stephen Covey

SCORE: 81%

OUTLINE: Habits that improve life and productivity.

REVIEW: IN this book Stephen Covey examines why it is that successful people seem to be able to achieve more than the average person and how they get so much done in the same amount of time. As well as being a productivity enhancer it also looks at how you can improve the quality of what you create or the work that you do. He stresses the importance of being proactive rather than reactive, how any job you take on should start with the end goal and to always try and think of a win-win scenario when dealing with situations.

He goes on to explain the value of being an effective listener to really be able to help solve problems and to prioritise by putting the first things first. It's a great read to encourage some new habits to implement on your path your higher productivity and general life enhancement.

THE INTERNATIONAL BESTSELLER

# THE MIRACLE MORNING

## THE **6 HABITS** THAT WILL TRANSFORM YOUR LIFE BEFORE **8AM**

### HAL ELROD

# Miracle Morning - Hal Elrod

SCORE: 96%

OUTLINE: Get shit done while others are still snoozing.

REVIEW:This is another 'game changer'. Listen, there is a very good reason that some of the worlds most successful people endorse an early start to the day with an immediate routine. Neuroscientists, clinical psychologists, globally successful entrepreneurs and athletes alike all wrote ,in the press, about the benefits of this lifestyle change. This book will help you usher in that change. Hal Elrod is attempting to lead a world movement, as well as selling books. If you decide to read this book and take on the Miracle Morning challenge you will not only find his practical tips useful but you will find that you will get social media support from strangers, globally! If you're struggling he has support communities, available free, on many digital platforms where others can help suggest solutions to your impossible obstacles that would get in the way of this routine.

I apply his advice when I do wake up and over time I've found that I have adjusted his routine slightly to fit better with my life. Give this book a read, give it a go, you might find your productivity go through the roof!

# The 4 Hour Work Week - Timothy Ferris

SCORE: 77%

OUTLINE: One way of escaping the 9-5.

REVIEW: A practical guide with cited references of how to outsource a lot of your current job roles and how to secure remote working. Detailed coverage of who, what, when, where, why and how on personal assistants, time management and how to avoid poor or low productivity. Great recommendations and further reading suggestions at the end of the book. Some of the book's principles are not applicable to all professions; for instance you may struggle to work remotely if you are a professional athlete, care giver, doctor, pilot or other professions that relies on your presence.

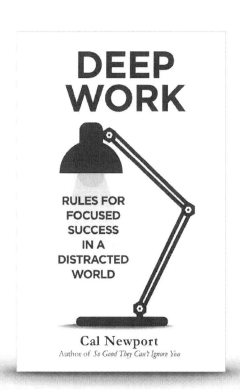

# DEEP WORK

**RULES FOR
FOCUSED
SUCCESS
IN A
DISTRACTED
WORLD**

## Cal Newport
Author of *So Good They Can't Ignore You*

# Deep Work - Cal Newport

SCORE: 80%

OUTLINE: Ideas, techniques and advice on how to work in a deep focused like manner.

REVIEW: The author talks about advice, particularly to benefit those in the creative industry, on how to perform deep work. There are obvious suggestions from switching off your smartphone all the way through to quitting all social media, electronic communication and even isolation from the outside world. The author highlights examples where people have achieved deep work before, how they have done it and the effects it can have emotionally , psychologically and physiologically. An interesting read especially if you have a big project that you want to work on and want some advice on how to do it.

# 14. ENTREPRENEURIALISM & BUSINESS.

*Creative and pragmatic inspirations and solutions.*

If you've already read the chapter on finance then this will be a great follow on to that if you have decided that you want to develop those ideas further. Equally, if you know someone, or feel yourself that you'd like to work for yourself rather than someone else, then the following books have some great inspiration on how such tasks can be done.

There are books that cover the conceptual idea of a start up in its early stage and take it all the way through to a globally successful company such as Paypal. The different authors cover how they fought through the obstacles that seemed impossible to defy and yet despite the odds go on to achieve success.

There are also examples of how dysfunctional leaders have inadvertently dragged down a successful company and all but killed it. You have examples of companies like Apple that under the right leadership thrived beyond any of the expected targets and how when they temporarily had the wrong leader at the helm they suffered. There is also examples of companies like Blackberry who tried to emulate Apple and in doing so stepped away from their core values, and customers, and went from a dominant market share, in the mobile industry, to that of one that was less than 1%. So there are a lot of lessons in here. The resource value of the books, when directly applied to your business, project or goal, are very valuable but they are equally as valuable, if not more so, when you apply the lessons into other disciplines of your life.

If you are thinking of making the leap into starting a business, or already have one and want to keep your mind sharp to the possibilities of change and improvement, then the books coming up will provide inspiration and insight into possible solutions. There are so many moving parts within a company, so many factors, people, rules, ethics, finances and more, and thinking you have them all sorted is at best naive and at worst fatal. One thing that is easy to do when reading business and entrepreneurial books is to criticise a manager, boss or CEO that we know and draw all the lessons from the book and highlight how we would have done it differently. The positive thing is that if you do go into business, or are already in it, then you can take the lessons from these books and model your own choices in a more informed manner.

You may have a vision of working your way up through the company and eventually becoming the CEO yourself. If that is the case then it's not going to be the following books alone that help you get there. Sure there might be some single books or concepts that you always return to but one of the trends you start to see again and again, within books of this type, is that the really effective business leaders, owners and star employees never stop learning and developing. So the game you play will be one of constant learning and development rather than a quick hack to get you the job you're after. They are always looking to improve themselves as well as their businesses and it is the long term thinking that breeds success.

The books that are in here will certainly highlight different management techniques. You may be an entrepreneur, a solo-preneur, a CEO, an employee or a wannabe of the above. The examples of not just management style but leadership, tactics, resolve, public relations and marketing will be of great use to you in shaping and moulding a future that you can sustain and thrive in whilst balancing ethics and profit.

All the knowledge contained in these books is predominantly illustrated in the work and business sphere but the lessons provided are transferable into personal life as well. Many of the authors will highlight that principles they have actioned within a company were indeed inspired from their personal lives or vice versa and that both business and home have seen positive changes and improvements as a result. Can you imagine having to run and control the finances of a tech start up? If you're all over that and some of that expertise rubs off on your home life you'd find that finances at home might also see an up turn and suddenly one of the biggest causes for family arguments has started to abate and leave space for more positive time together. Beware though! This is not a magic elixir.

For every successful person that seems to effortlessly transfer their business skills into their personal life there is another example of a person that does not. Tiger Woods, Ariana Huffington and President Kennedy are just three of the cited examples where they were public hailed as heroes in their disciplines, but privately lead lives that were destructive and immoral. It is far less destructive to learn from their errors and avoid them than it is to blindly commit them yourself.

The decision making ideas, problem solving techniques, communication improvements, resourcefulness ideas and character traits within these books are nothing short of inspirational! Take all the good bits and make yourself the business person you want to be.

| | |
|---|---|
| Zero to One | Peter Thiel |
| If You're Not First You're Last | Grant Cardone |
| Loosing My Virginity | Richard Branson |
| Scrum | Jeff Sutherland |
| The Infinite Game | Simon Sinek |
| The Thank You Economy | Gary Veynerchuck |

# ZERO

## TO

## ONE

### NOTES ON STARTUPS,
#### OR
### HOW TO BUILD THE FUTURE

## PETER THIEL
### WITH BLAKE MASTERS

'That rare thing: a concise, thought-provoking
book on entrepreneurship' THE TIMES

# Zero To One - Peter Thiel, Blake Masters

SCORE: 80%

OUTLINE: In a world of imitations, mock ups and copies, 'Zero to One' highlights the significance of actually being the first.

REVIEW: The author looks at a few of the companies he started as case studies including PAYAL and co-founding SPACE X. This is essentially a 'dos and don'ts' guide to starting up a company/ business or movement when you're acting as a lone entrepreneur. There are discussions around how to form a company, the importance of clearly defined roles and who to look for when you are recruiting. This book is probably best placed in the hands of someone who has a clear passion and vision for a product, or service, and needs some advice on the first steps of launching and distribution.

# If You're Not First You're Last - Grant Cardone

SCORE: 77%

OUTLINE: Another kick up the arse from Cardone.

REVIEW: In this book the author looks at being first, as in first in the customers eyes, rather than first in a race, in order to succeed in times of difficulty and triumph. You need to flex or die. Stay the same and you'll fade, don't deny when you're suffering. Keep your head up, your mind strong, and look for change and opportunity. It's delivered with all the enthusiasm you'd expect from Grant Cardone, if you're not familiar with him that means a lot of energy, and he has some sound advice on how to build and protect a business.

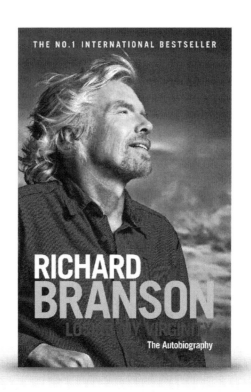

THE NO.1 INTERNATIONAL BESTSELLER

**RICHARD BRANSON**

The Autobiography

# Loosing My Virginity -Richard Branson

SCORE: 84%

OUTLINE: Bransons account of starting in business.

REVIEW: Interesting read about how he started and surprising about the number of financial decisions that, seemingly by luck, worked out for him. Importantly he notes that he worked hard and he embraced challenges as feedback that he was developing. His side of the British Airways and Virgin Atlantic ongoing battle is very insightful.  There are a whole bunch of business titles by Branson that could all be read in this chapter and they all offer real life insight to how he has managed, developed, hired, bought, sold and restructured businesses.

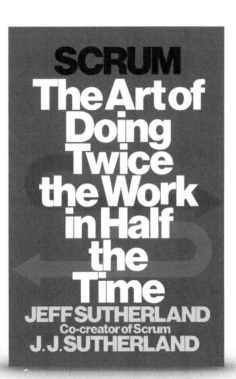

# SCRUM

## The Art of Doing Twice the Work in Half the Time

**JEFF SUTHERLAND**
Co-creator of Scrum
**J. J. SUTHERLAND**

# Scrum - Jeff Sutherland

SCORE: 77%

OUTLINE: An unorthodox leadership/management technique model.

REVIEW: 'Scrum' is a book that looks at a management style differing to that of conventional management and project leadership through a waterfall approach. Scrum empowers team members to do what they want and when they want and to take ownership of a project and all work holistically towards the same goal. The book has some great insights about where and when 'Scrum' has been implemented, what 'Scrum' conceptualises and in the appendices looks at how to implement 'Scrum'. The basic concept is that you all work together at the same time moving one line forward to produce the minimum viable product which offers the max value for your customers and you don't worry about producing a polished final product. The aim is to give the customer the biggest valued item as quickly as possible and to refine and perfect your product in many iterations, the same way that perhaps someone like Apple used to do at the beginning where they launched a minimum viable product and then perfected it on the feedback of the first users.

THE
INFINITE
GAME
**THE
INFINITE
GAME
SIMON
SINEK**
THE
INFINITE
GAME
THE
INFINITE

THE BESTSELLING AUTHOR OF
**START WITH WHY**
AND
**LEADERS EAT LAST**

# The Infinite Game - Simon Sinek

SCORE: 99%

OUTLINE: The long game is for the real 'winners'.

REVIEW: This is by far one of the best books I have read on business, leadership style and management of a strategic objective of a company. Do not be fooled though into thinking that this only applies to business. It does not and there are analogies in the book that can be drawn into your personal life, political career, sporting endeavours, military campaign or even parenting style, are abundant. The essential message is that if you are fighting for a short term win rather than playing the long game then you are on borrowed time and you are playing a finite game rather than an infinite game. Companies in our current time do not last like they used to. A business used to last several decades, not several years and the author analyses, with case studies and examples, why this happens and how shareholders pressure, short sighted statistic chasing CEOs and the wrong inherited and entrenched culture can lead to failure. This book has so much useful content that I think it's difficult to overstate how valuable of a read it is. It's certainly worth a re-read as well.

NEW YORK TIMES BESTSELLER

"You owe it to yourself to read this book!"
—Tony Hsieh, Chief Executive Officer, Zappos.com

# THE
# THANK YOU
# ECONOMY

## gary vay•ner•chuk

Author of the *New York Times* Bestseller *Crush It!*

# The Thank You Economy - Gary Vaynerchuck

SCORE: 83%

OUTLINE: A book endorsing the social media trend and its value to businesses.

REVIEW: Gary V highlights how, where, why and who should be getting involved in social media and how, importantly, it can be used to complement a marketing campaign rather than replacing the advertising industry. Unfortunately the book is already a little out of date and the author explains at the end that if you are 'reading this in 2015 he will be proved right or wrong'. Well 2015 is in the past so I suppose that really the book goes a long way to endorsing the fact that Gary V was right and that perhaps what he is saying now, about the future, also may be correct. He is a very energetic guy who has built up a huge following and if you want to find him on the web it will not take you long at all.

# 15. CONFIDENCE.

*You're probably already ready, here's your reassurance.*

There's no way you can do that, right? It's not possible is it? Surely not. Well not for you but that other person they can do it. Yeah sure. But they were born with he ability to do it. They were lucky and that s why they're so confident right? BULL SHIT.

World champs aren't just born, CEOs, Actors, Presidents and acclaimed writers aren't just born. They work at it. They hone their craft and over time they eventually get positive feedback and that positive feedback in turn, like a self fulfilling prophecy, then gives them the confidence to keep going, pushing harder, trying new things and not worrying if they have to fail at something a thousand times just to get it right once.

Sometimes, the one thing that stops you doing all that, the thing that stops you even trying in the first place is the lack of confidence. Well, help is at hand. The books in this chapter can be quite specific about how to help nurture confidence in someone or in yourself and I expect this will be one of the first read chapters by a lot of people. You are not alone if you feel like you do not have a lot of confidence. In fact you are joined by many successful people who either once felt the same or in many cases still do feel that way despite their success and notoriety.

I'll just point out a few things here before letting you go into the reviews and then picking out your most suitable read. Firstly, whether you think you can or you think you can't, you're right either way. By this I mean that if you just *think* you can do something you'll probably be comfortable trying it and risking failure, even publicly, enduring attempt after attempt because you'll have a notion that what you are trying to achieve is possible. If you *think* you *can't* (can't is the real c word) do something then you're probably not even going to try. So if you genuinely believe in what you're trying to achieve then you owe it to that mission, project, belief, etc to start getting into the ' I *think* I can' mindset.

Secondly, is it you or is it someone else saying you can't do it, or shouldn't do it, or won't do it? If it's someone else then this is great news! What?!?! If someone else imposes on to you that you're not able to achieve something and that crushes your confidence then I'll let you into a secret that the authors in this chapter will validate... people who tell others that they can't are normally just projecting their own inability and inadequate feelings on to you because they are intimidated by your idea and how your success will make them feel as a result. If your competition tells you that there's no way you can run a mile in under 4 mins then that belief will remain the norm. If you, like Roger Banister, have the confidence that it can be done, and he did it despite what everyone said, then suddenly your competition is fucked. They are left behind and they feel bad and that's why they impose their beliefs on to you; to protect themselves.

On a positive note where you trail blaze ahead you will inspire others like you to follow in your wake and suddenly everyone will believe it can be done and soon loads of other people will be doing it. So kudos for you for blazing the way.

Oh and if it's you that is getting in your own way then take a listen to 'The Imposter Cure'. All the self doubt in the World is covered in this book by a lady who has been in the very same position but found a few ways of working through it and pushing through.

Everyone is so concerned with what other people think of them. We all need to let this go and I think with age that is something that becomes easier, but you don't have the luxury of waiting until you get old to develop the confidence to do something because by then, you guessed it, it will be too late. In your teens and twenties all you think about is what other people think about you and how to fit in. In your thirties and forties you don't give a shit and you just get on with what you need to do anyway. In your fifties you realise that no one ever really gave a shit about you anyway as they were way too busy worrying about what other people thought of them. Sometimes you just need to accept the fact that you are unique and individual and if you weren't, and we were all the same, then this planet would be one boring fucking place to live.

Sarah Knight will tell you to just be yourself. Have confidence in your decisions and what you want to do. You don't have to conform to some societal norm and as long as you're not physically or psychologically hurting anyone then, probably, no-one will give a shit anyway.

So take your project, however big it is, and risk a little failure, perhaps even some humiliation, to get it done and get it going.

Get that product out there and get some feedback on it and then make it better with future iterations. The important thing is to get it out there in the first place and people will believe in, and invest in, your 'minimum viable product' if it is something that you believe will work.

A perfect case in point is this book. Is it perfect? Fuck no! Does it do the job the I want it to? Hopefully, yes. Are you going to tell me about all the errors in it? I hope so, I can correct them and make the next version better. Do I care if you think ill of me because I have missed splleing, punctuation and grammar errors No! (See what I did there?) I could send it to a professional publishers but its quicker for me to get it out there myself and I doubt they would publish it anyway. Have a little, or a lot, of faith in yourself and your idea.

If you still need a little more help after reading all these books then I can suggest one last thing . Take the confident words of JAY Z and repeat them over and over in your head until you cant help but believe they are your own. Repeat after me: This ain't a tall order this is nothing to me, difficult takes a day, impossible takes a week. You can do it, you are worthy! Ready, GO!

| | |
|---|---|
| Failing Forward | John Maxwell |
| Start Now Get Perfect Later | Rob Moore |
| The Subtle Art of Not Giving A F**k | Mark Manson |
| You Do You | Sarah Knight |
| Anyone Can Do It | Duncan Banytyne |
| You Are a Badass | Jen Sincero |
| Trusting Yourself | MJ Ryan |
| The Imposter Cure | Jessamy Hibberd |

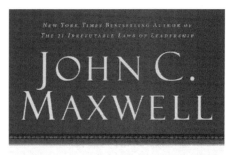

# Failing Forward - John Maxwell

SCORE: 79%

OUTLINE: Welcome failure into your life and use its potential instead of fearing it.

REVIEW: John Maxwell gives lots of examples of how you can utilise a failure and benefit from it. This is valuable for those that are really concerned about failing and probably 'reaffirming' for those who don't concern themselves with the risk of failure. The author illustrates how he left school afraid of failure as the education establishment breeds that fear into you. Then he highlights how he suffered from failure and how he got over it. He gives examples of how anyone can learn from their mistakes and can embrace failure to help with their confidence in getting ahead. Essentially he makes failure his friend and uses it to his strength and shows how anyone else can as well.

LIFE GOALS

TASK ONE

☑ Start Now

TASK TWO

☑ Get Perfect Later

☑ Rob Moore

Bestselling author of
LIFE LEVERAGE and MONEY

# Start Now Get Perfect Later - Rob Moore

SCORE: 90%

OUTLINE: Rob's encouragement to just start now, forget perfection, and work towards excellence as you go along.

REVIEW: In this book Rob Moore looks at people's levels of procrastination, why and how it manifests and how to get around it. If you know someone who is always waiting to perfect something before launching it then you could really help them by giving this book. Rob looks at the benefits of releasing a minimum viable product that serves your customer/audience and then perfecting it later with the only exceptions to this being a surgeon or a pilot in a highly skilled job. But even they will perfect skills in time and are not perfect when they start. There are a few links, but pertinent and useful ones, to Robs other books and these are plugged in a way that are useful rather than heavily salesman-like. Don't let perfection get in the way of your aim to get something out there to the world that you think would be of value. iPhones don't go out to market perfectly ready, evidenced by their constant software upgrade requirements, and Apple is one of the most cash rich companies on the planet, so there's no need for you to wait for perfect either.

# The Subtle Art of Not Giving A F*ck - Mark Manson

SCORE: 83%

OUTLINE: Why it's a good idea to care less about everything but still care about something.

REVIEW: The author comes up with some sound advice about how a lot of pressure is self inflicted and how the stresses of these pressures can be counter productive or intuitive and therefore often it is just your mind getting in the way of your success. The chapters are split quite well into applications of different concerns you may have and there is sound advice on how to improve these situations. There are personal accounts that the author has experienced and illustrations of famous examples where the likes of The Beatles, Metallica, Romeo and Juliet and many more may have implemented some of the advice presented in the book. Certainly worth a listen and the key thing that I would take away is that when you really want something, like the dream wife, it's often there in plain sight and can only really be found when you try to not give a fuck.

A
no-f**ks
given guide

# You *Do* You

how to be who you are
and use what you've got
to get what you want

## Sarah Knight

'The anti-guru'
*Observer*

The bestselling author of
*The Life-Changing Magic of Not Giving a F**k*
and *Get Your Sh*t Together*

# You Do You - Sarah Knight

SCORE: 91%

OUTLINE: Sarah's trilogy stating: Be yourself. Fuck 'em.

REVIEW: After 'The Art Of Not Giving a f**k' and 'Get Your S**t Together.', the author has come up with a book that simply exclaims that you are yourself and you should be un-apologetically so. It's time to ditch the concerns of social conformity , family pressure and friends assumptions of what you should do. Be selfish when you need to, organise your stuff and don't apologise for that shabby old T-shirt you like to wear. It looks great on you. A fantastic read not only for a confidence boost but to help you feel validated about your choices.

UPDATED

## DUNCAN BANNATYNE

From an Ice Cream Van to Dragons' Den

## ANYONE CAN DO IT

MY STORY

# Anyone Can Do It - Duncan Bannatyne

SCORE: 91%

OUTLINE: The brief history a UK entrepreneur.

REVIEW: Duncan Bannatyne is a 'rags to riches' UK entrepreneur. In this book you can learn about his story and why he thinks anyone is capable of achieving what he has done. He says he started business life late, at 30, and quickly made huge sums of money by adding value to projects from serving ice cream, building care homes and taking over leisure gym chains. It's a very frank and open account and I like that it's not polished. He narrates the audio book himself and the account feels very genuine. At its core the book imparts that if he can do it so can you. Be confident, have the courage, take action.

#1 *NEW YORK TIMES* BESTSELLER
TWO MILLION COPIES IN PRINT!

# YOU
are a
# BADASS

HOW TO STOP DOUBTING
YOUR GREATNESS
AND START LIVING AN
AWESOME LIFE
JEN SINCERO
WITH A NEW FOREWORD BY THE AUTHOR

# You Are A BADASS - Jen Sincero

SCORE: 90%

OUTLINE: 'You Are a Badass' is the self-help audiobook for people who desperately want to improve their lives but don't want to get busted doing it.

REVIEW: The author will help talk you out of your own negative/ internal self fulfilling downward spiral. Take her advice; we are all humans and anyone is capable of almost anything. The only thing stopping you is you. There are some great tips on how you can quell the negative thoughts that sometimes stop you from achieving your full potential. The narrator has got a great sense of humour, doesn't take herself too seriously and at the same time tackles a fairly serious subject. A great book to listen to with someone else who you think doubts themselves a little too much and doesn't quite realise how good they are!

**trusting yourself**

**Growing Your Self-Awareness,
Self-Confidence, and Self-Reliance**

M J RYAN

Author of *Attitudes of Gratitude* and *The Power of Patience*

# Trusting Yourself - M.J.Ryan

SCORE: 82%

OUTLINE: Ways to learn to trust yourself more and relax about it.

REVIEW: A book that highlights how many unhappy or uneasy feelings, that consume a whole load of energy, time and effort, may just be caused by our worst enemy; ourselves. Notice it and let it go. Take a stoic view of it and if you want to change something then change it but if it's out of your sphere of influence then why worry if it rains? This book could be the read that helps you, or someone you know, on their way and help them to finally take action on their aims.

# THE

YOU ARE NOT A FRAUD.

# IMPOSTER

YOU DESERVE SUCCESS.

# CURE

YOU CAN BELIEVE IN YOURSELF.

**How to stop feeling
like a fraud and escape
the mind-trap of
imposter syndrome**

Dr Jessamy Hibberd

# The Imposter Cure - Dr Jessamy Hibberd

SCORE: 83%

OUTLINE: How to avoid imposter syndrome.

REVIEW: I listened to the start of this book with my wife and we both know it is something that she identifies with closely. Listening to it together certainly helped my empathy with her feelings and to try and ask questions about how things make her feel rather than just trying to reassure her. I think the point to note is that if you don't, or at least seldom feel like an imposter in your role, then you'll find it difficult to appreciate how much it affects those that do. Listening to the book will identify ways to help people who do constantly feel like they are an imposter, that they are not good enough or that they feel that they don't deserve what it is they are aiming for. There is some practicable advice and tips in here that would hopefully help ease the negative feeling and help you move through the fear.

# 16. BONUS CHAPTER: INSIGHT.

*Mind opening information across incredible subjects.*

When I started writing this guide to self help there were books along the way that I just could not leave out. I whittled the main 15 chapters down to 100 books and the following titles just had to be included and so I came up with this bonus chapter. These are some truly eye opening books that I am confident you will love. In compiling these books together, in their own chapter, my aim is to highlight how interesting it is to gain clarity and understanding of someone, or somethings, specific situation and the challenges they face and the factors that affect them. I have chosen books that illustrate accessible environments so as to keep the information relevant. These books offer insight into a whole host of scenarios that I have never considered and I hope for you they do the same.

There is some great benefit in developing our own insight. You may be able to do this in your specific field of expertise , perhaps relating to your career, or you may like to just develop it generally and read around an array of subjects. So how do you become more insightful? You can see it as a practice where you deliberately focus your curiosity on a topic that interests you and try to disprove any assumptions that you have. Ultimately you can explore content, cultures, meanings, behaviours and other peoples accounts to aggregate your knowledge and combine it with how it makes you feel as well. It's almost a combination of heart, head and facts to help broaden your perspective, add to your reasoning around decision making and inspire motivation to change when necessary.

Someone can tell you in five minutes something that has taken them a life time to learn. And that has a phenomenal amount of potential if you actually stop to listen. These lessons and insights might only normally be passed on to a few people who are close to the person holding that wisdom and thankfully books mean that this message can be picked up by many people at any time.

The insights into people's lives, ideas, careers and experiences can be absolutely mind opening. Sometimes what you hear or read will leave you absolutely speechless, sometimes in tears and sometimes in hysterical laughter. This is what the Insight chapter is about. They are the books that you absolutely have to tell your friends about, to read, to learn from, because the ideas and concepts are just unbelievable.

There are books in here that will make you realise that global wars, pandemics and political influence are less controlled by people and more dependant on the land you stand on and the seas and mountains that surround you. You'll see how pioneering battles are now fought on keyboards and not on war fields.

This chapter covers philosophies learnt in tragedy that bring positivity to millions, how the loss of one man's wife lead to a global movement that saved hundreds of others who would have been a similar situation. On the medical theme there are books that show the insight and bravery of people operating selflessly in the harshest environments and then another book hilariously illustrating the struggles of junior doctors in the UK .

Some people are smart professionals but it's amazing to learn how, as humans, we are really quite dumb in the grand scheme of things. That message is repeated in 'You Are Not So Smart' which covers some of the traits in human behavioural psychology that make you realise why we sometimes do, say and suggest the daftest things and what then makes us actually go ahead with them as a result.

The Insight chapter is intended to be educational and entertaining. It's not directly about applying techniques to your life that will make you the next millionaire. It's about showing you a collection of individuals and their concepts that might just make you stop and think; "Could that work in my life?". It might just inspire you to change something that seems small but something that one day could do something as powerful as save the life of someone, or of millions of people. A big statement, sure, but don't take my word for it, read the reviews, pick a book, sit back and drink it all in.

Black Box Thinking                 Matthew Syed

Humans                             Tom Philips

This is Going to Hurt              Adam Kay

Prisoners of Geography            Tim Marshall

War Doctor                         David Knott

Checklist Manifesto               Atol Gwande

Countdown to Zero Hour Day        Kim Zotter

You Are Not So Smart              David McRaney

The Secret Barrister              Jack Hawkins

Catching Stardust                 Natalie Starsky

81 Days Below Zero                Brian Murphy

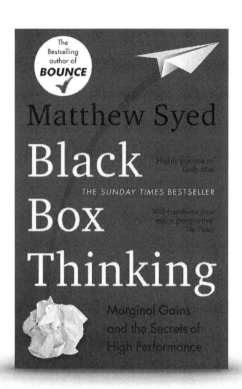

# Black Box Thinking - Matthew Syed

SCORE: 95%

OUTLINE: Turn your flair into growth opportunity.

REVIEW: This book is impossible to over-sell. Matthew Syed has written several books and this is his greatest. The book looks at how the aviation industry uses failure as a learning opportunity and how pinnacle that philosophy is in contributing towards the highest safety standards. In aviation it is safety that the term 'Black Box Thinking' relates to. However you can apply the term to many industries and this mindset of 'Black Box Thinking' is illustrated in this book with fantastic case studies. Stories of how Team Sky used it to improve their success as well as how it can massively impact the heath care system to reduce unnecessary deaths.

I am privileged enough to know the Pilot involved in the story that the book focuses on at the beginning. The author highlights the event that the pilot was involved with and rightfully illustrates how the reactions of the pilot are at the pinnacle level of the 'Black Box Thinking' mindset. This book gives phenomenal insight into the life of a man whose drive and passion, to selflessly improve an industry, unrelated to his own, has led to not only global but also noble infamy (Twitter @MartinBromiley).

# HUMANS

## A Brief History of How We F*cked It All Up

TOM PHILLIPS

# Humans - Tom Phillips

SCORE: 79%

OUTLINE: How humans have fucked up in the past.

REVIEW: The author examines a whole bunch of things that have been ruined in the past, including governments, human endeavour, colonialism and Hitler, to name but a few. The anecdotes are told in a very informal manner, which at first might appear a bit too jovial, but actually become very funny. The great thing about this book is that you can identify failures of people, powers, nature etc and then attempt to apply those learnings to issues that you may be struggling with. And the book is informative to boot!

# This Is Going To Hurt - Adam Kay

SCORE: 90%

OUTLINE: Hilarious, frightening and insightful look at a junior doctor in their early career.

REVIEW: In this, frankly, fascinating book the author, and narrator, covers some of his funny, gruesome, heartbreaking and inspirational stories. The scenarios cited in this junior doctor notes give a raw and realistic illustration of the trials and tribulations of our UK based NHS doctors. It will probably make you call a doctor and thank them for their work. Amazing book. Hilarious. Entertaining and educational.

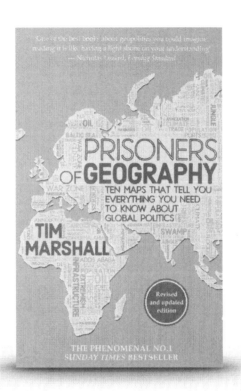

# Prisoners Of Geography - Tim Marshall

SCORE: 90%

OUTLINE: Mountains and rivers may be more powerful than any political power.

REVIEW: This book details a lot of the geopolitics that has happened in the World in the past and that could happen in the future not only on earth but beyond the realms of this planet. It looks at how crucial a point geography actually plays and that despite world powers sometimes expanding, and in many cases over stretching, it will be geography that eventually settles where border lines lie. Particularly interesting is the conflict caused over the boundaries of countries that were artificially drawn up many years ago by European explorers in, say for instance, the Middle East and how these lines are fairly pointless, not respected, and continue to cause conflict.

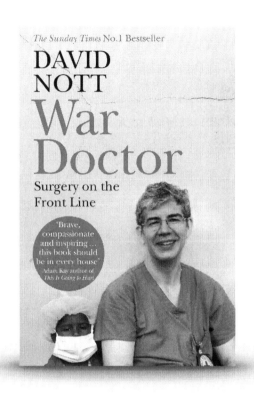

*The Sunday Times* No.1 Bestseller

# DAVID
# NOTT

# War
# Doctor

## Surgery on the
## Front Line

'Brave,
compassionate
and inspiring ...
this book should
be in every house'
Adam Kay author of
*This Is Going to Hurt*

# War Doctor - David Nott

SCORE: 75%

OUTLINE: Accounts of a front line medic.

REVIEW: In this book Nott covers, in chronological, order his career story. The choices, decisions and judgements he has made along the way. Stories of bravery where he has continued to operate in hospitals under attack and how he has revolutionised medical techniques in a time of necessity, and all as a volunteer! He covers how his life has originally left him lonely until meeting his now wife and what she has to subsequently adapt to within their marriage. It's a fascinating book and if you've been to a war zone and thought what was going on was pretty fucked up, and I have, then you'll soon be dumbfounded by his accounts of issues in Somalia and Libya.

# Checklist Manifesto - Atul Gawande

SCORE: 78%

OUTLINE: Aviation checklists introduced to other disciplines.

REVIEW: In this book the author looks at the different industries that have tried to take on aviation checklists. The author himself is a medic and describes how hospitals alone can benefit vastly from the use of checklist and how sometimes their integration needs to be done with all the staff rather than just the lead department clinicians. There is an interesting case study about how they take the checklist manifesto project to different countries all over the world with different levels of affluence to see how the integration of the check this will benefit the relative hospitals. It is a very insightful read and makes you consider how, even in your own personal life, a checklist, at the appropriate points, may yield huge benefits.

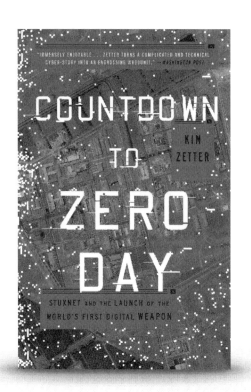

"IMMENSELY ENJOYABLE... ZETTER TURNS A COMPLICATED AND TECHNICAL
CYBER-STORY INTO AN ENGROSSING WHODUNIT." —WASHINGTON POST

# COUNTDOWN

KIM
ZETTER

## TO

# ZERO

# DAY

STUXNET AND THE LAUNCH OF THE
WORLD'S FIRST DIGITAL WEAPON

# Countdown To Zero Day - Kim Zetter

SCORE: 75%

OUTLINE: A look into cyber warfare and it's impacts.

REVIEW: This book looks at how cyber warfare has been utilised in the past and how it may be utilised in the future. Like the Americans disrupting Iranian nuclear enrichment programs, after failing diplomacy talks, that were discovered by tech companies in the East. It's fascinating how the electronic warfare platform can be used to sabotage your enemy, how once you start these acts you have shown your hand at your capabilities and in doing so identified yourself as the attacker. It's an advanced set of systems and principles to get your head around but, no doubt, principles that will become far more obvious in hindsight. It's amazing to realise all the things that go on in this world that we have no knowledge of and perhaps no concern upon as a consequence, despite how important they actually are.

# You Are Not So Smart- David McRaney

SCORE: 75%

OUTLINE: Many reasons why we're not as smart as we think.

REVIEW: If you think you make educated decisions then, in the words of the author, you're not so smart. It's all about everyday lies that we tell ourselves that we believe in that are in a lot of cases a load of bollocks! These lies though often keep us sane and the author suggests he's not trying to be offensive but just enlighten you as to some things we do that really are unnecessary. He discusses brand loyalty, confirmation bias, hindsight bias and why you probably have too many Facebook friends. I love the bit on brand loyalty which illustrates you don't buy a brand again because it's reliable, think of all the things that are wrong with your current brand, you in fact are attempting to justify your first decision to bond with the brand and if you keep going back then you can't be wrong. Surely? A very insightful read.

# The
## SECRET
# Barrister

Stories of the Law
and How It's Broken

'Eye-opening, damning and hilarious'
Tim Shapman, author of Fall Out and All Out War

# The Secret Barrister - Jack Hawkins

SCORE: 77%

OUTLINE: An inside look into the Great British justice system.

REVIEW: This book is a really insightful look into the legal world. The author offers their opinion on the current fledgling state of the UK justice system as a result of poor politics and austerity measures. There are some fascinating cases that will have you gasping as well as some audacious criminals that re-offend time and again and get away with it, scot-free, by playing the system. Also if your middle classed there are some eye opening considerations that will have you very much worried for your future especially if you find yourself in court!

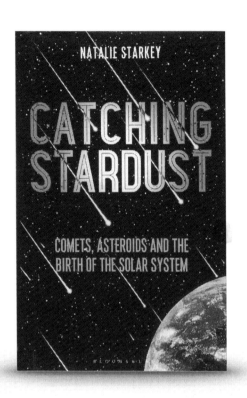

# Catching Stardust - Natalie Starkey

SCORE: 78%

OUTLINE: A look into Space dust, its mystery and mastery.

REVIEW: Natalie Starkey works with the likes of NASA, ESA and other worldly space bodies to explore the origins of star dust and its make up. In the book she looks at a lot of the factors that can affect its collection, origin, composition, life and its findings. She talks of the success of relative recent space missions and gives great insight into just how long they take, how they actually happen and who the people are that run them. The figures involved in the book can be mind bending but the author does well to contextualise them and make more fathomable measurements in the reader's eyes. It will certainly give you some perspective on how humans relate to the grand scheme of things.

THE INCREDIBLE SURVIVAL STORY
OF A WORLD WAR II PILOT IN
ALASKA'S FROZEN WILDERNESS

81
DAYS
BELOW
ZERO

BRIAN MURPHY
WITH TOULA VLAHOU

# 81 Days Below Zero - Brian Murphy

SCORE: 78%

OUTLINE: A survival story based on luck, determination and deliberate thought.

REVIEW: This book is about a WWII airman that crashed in Alaska during a trials sortie and was the only surviving member of his crew. What happens when your rescue mission never finds you or your wreckage and you are hundreds of miles from anyone in the frozen tundra? You walk out. Alone. And that's what he did. A lot of luck enroute and some ingenuity get this airman out and back home. A great story about determination and how sometimes rules are not always best blindly followed in a life and death scenario.

# FINAL THOUGHTS.

So you have got to the end of the book. Congratulations! I hope that you have some use in this book as a guide to helping you find your way through the thousands upon thousands of books available within the self help genre. Whilst writing this book I have been listening to more and more titles and I continue to review them individually on my website www.ReadLearnInspire.com. I will hopefully one day produce an even larger guide that encompasses even more and if you stay in touch I'll be sure to let you know when it comes out. You can follow me on instagram as well at @ReadLearnInspire. I hope by now this book is dog-eared and well used. I hope that you have written notes, doodled in it and inspired yourself to action to improve an area of your life that you really wanted to try and get on top of.

I would advise you not to overwhelm yourself with the challenge of change. Humans seem to be innately drawn to homogeny and the safety of comfortable routine. So if you are stepping out of your comfort zone and your schedule then you'll probably find more success taking one step at a time. Learn through trial and error which suggestions in the title work for you and if its appropriate offer help to someone else by highlighting just how it could work for them. Recommending this book might be one of the most helpful things you can do and it will enable me to continue working on future titles as well.

The biggest key to any of the help you'll read about in the titles that I reviewed is taking ACTION. It can not be stressed enough. If all you do is read about what can help you and you don't actually follow through and commit to some level of change then, yes, you have developed your knowledge, which is no bad thing, but you haven't yet developed your situation. If you study too earn good grades or you go to work to earn money then you do it in the faith that someone will reward you for your effort and time. When you are developing yourself there is not always that guarantee that we are normally require to commit our effort towards something. It does take a little faith and trust and it nearly always take some courage and conviction. I can't absolutely guarantee you'll be better off for trying some of the advice within the books out but I can tell you that a load of the tips and tricks, over time, have helped me develop in health, happiness, finance, purpose and, most importantly, as a more well rounded and open minded individual.

It's not always easy to persuade your 'younger self' that they could benefit from a little extra reading. You won't get far standing on your soap box and preaching to people the way of the world through personal development books. Sometimes I think its best to just leave a crumb trail of obvious evidence along your own path of development. Read, Learn and Inspire

# THANK YOU.

Firstly thank you to you for reading this book and helping yourself. I urge you to do the most important thing and take action to achieve what ever it is that you want or indeed to help others who you think may benefit from any of the knowledge in this book.

I'd like to say thanks to all of the authors of the books that have offered me inspiration and to Audible for creating a platform where someone as simple as me can read, learn and hopefully inspire others.

Thank you to my friends and family who I have sent many, MANY versions of this book to look over and review and that have offered me guidance and feedback. Pinot G, Ade, Masser, JT, Pink face and Jeddy are life long friends that support my ambition rather than dissuade me. My brothers and sisters Daniel, Danielle, Lewis, Sam, Emma, Chris and Tom who always listen to me talking about the latest book I have read and humour me with their interest.

My parents Roger and Gill, Beverley and Martin, Barbara and Tim who support my ambition and who I didn't even tell I was writing this book. SURPRISE! I wrote a book.

Thank you to the accountability team at S.T.A.M.I.N.A. Ben Mensah, Callum Black and Jatinder Ubhi who always support my ideas and keep me on track. They have introduced me to titles in this book that have changed my life. Their regular accountability keeps me going ,their vision helps me solve problems that baffle me and their friendship is something that I hope never stops getting stronger.

Special thanks to Natalie Moist who offered to read and edit this book whilst graciously battling some pretty shitty cancer. A life long friend that is now offering hope and inspiration others taking on the BIG C! @missiontoremission.

Finally a HUGE THANK YOU to my amazing wife! Jenny always listens to me when I am rabbiting on about what I have just learnt in another book and she even seems interested in it. She is endlessly supportive of every idea I have and she is the absolute centre of my life. Jen, thank you, I love you.

THIS AIN'T A TALL ORDER,
IT'S NOTHING TO ME,
DIFFICULT TAKES A DAY,
IMPOSSIBLE TAKES A WEEK.


JAY Z

THE END.

Printed in Poland
by Amazon Fulfillment
Poland Sp. z o.o., Wrocław

62426416R10186